ANTHROPOLOGICAL PAPERS

MUSEUM OF ANTHROPOLOGY, UNIVERSITY OF MICHIGAN

NO. 64

WĀSIṬA IN A LEBANESE CONTEXT SOCIAL EXCHANGE AMONG VILLAGERS AND OUTSIDERS

BY

FREDERICK CHARLES HUXLEY

ANN ARBOR, MICHIGAN
1978

Printed in the
United States of America

CONTENTS

List of Figures v
List of Maps vii
List of Plates vii
Acknowledgments ix

I. INTRODUCTION AND THEORETICAL BACKGROUND 1
II. ETHNOGRAPHY OF FIELD SITE 19
III. PSYCHOLINGUISTIC EXPERIMENT 57
IV. CONCLUSION 115

Appendixes 121
Bibliography 167

LIST OF FIGURES

1. Segmentary Kinship Organization 6
2. Taxonomy of Relationships Based on Social Exchange 17
3. Socio-Economic Classes in Barouk 49
4. Cross-Tabulation of Self-Placement (SP) and Researcher's Placement (RP) of Households 50
5. Groupings of Arabic Terms Used by Respondents into Self-Placement Categories 52
6. Cross-Tabulation of Respondents' Choices about Influential People in Barouk (IPB) with Researcher's Placements (RP) of Village Households . . . 53
7. Table of Income Distribution in Lebanon in 1959-60 53
8. Lorenz Curve of Disposable Income in Lebanon Generally in 1959-60 and in Barouk in 1974 55
9. Selected Voting Returns by Wards 61
10. List of Arabic Terms Chosen for the Psycholinguistic Experiment 64
11. Similarity Matrix for Free Sorts 68
12. Free-Sort Diagrams 69
13. Test for Significant Difference between All Subjects' Fixed Sorts and Free Sorts for "Persons between Whom There Is Economic Exchange" 72
14. Test for Significant Difference between All Subjects' Fixed Sorts and Free Sorts for "Persons between Whom There Is Political Exchange" 73
15. Test for Significant Difference between All Subjects' Fixed Sorts and Free Sorts for "Persons between Whom There Is Mutual Social Exchange" 74
16. Test For Significant Difference between All Subjects' Fixed Sorts and Free Sorts for "Higher Statuses" among "Persons between Whom There Is Economic Exchange" 76
17. Test for Significant Difference between All Subjects' Fixed Sorts and Free Sorts for "Lower Statuses" among "Persons between whom There Is Economic Exchange" 77
18. Test for Significant Difference between All Subjects' Fixed Sorts and Free Sorts for "Higher Statuses" among "Persons between Whom There Is Political Exchange" 78

19. Test for Significant Difference between All Subjects' Fixed Sorts and Free Sorts for "Lower Statuses" among "Persons between Whom There Is Political Exchange" 79
20. Tentative Labeling of Clusters on the Diameter Diagram 81
21. English Glosses for the Tentative Arabic Labels 81
22. Test for Significant Difference between Lower, Middle, and Upper Class Subgroups' Fixed Sorts and Free Sorts for "Persons between Whom There Is Economic Exchange" 84
23. Test for Significant Difference between Lower, Middle, and Upper Class Subgroups' Fixed Sorts and Free Sorts for "Persons between Whom There Is Political Exchange" 86
24. Test for Significant Difference between Lower, Middle, and Upper Class Subgroups' Fixed Sorts and Free Sorts for "Persons between Whom There Is Mutual Social Exchange" 88
25. Test for Significant Difference between Lower, Middle, and Upper Class Subgroups' Fixed Sorts and Free Sorts for "Higher Statuses" among "Persons between Whom There Is Economic Exchange" 90
26. Test for Significant Difference between Lower, Middle, and Upper Class Subgroups' Fixed Sorts and Free Sorts for "Lower Statuses" among "Persons between Whom There Is Economic Exchange" 92
27. Test for Significant Difference between Lower, Middle, and Upper Class Subgroups' Fixed Sorts and Free Sorts for "Higher Statuses" among "Persons between Whom There is Political Exchange" 94
28. Test for Significant Difference between Lower, Middle, and Upper Class Subgroups' Fixed Sorts and Free Sorts for "Lower Statuses" among "Persons between Whom There is Political Exchange" 96
29. Test for Significant Difference between Younger, Middle-Aged, and Older Subgroups' Fixed Sorts and Free Sorts for "Persons between Whom There Is Economic Exchange" 98
30. Test for Significant Difference between Younger, Middle-Aged, and Older Subgroups' Fixed Sorts and Free Sorts for "Persons between Whom There Is Political Exchange" 100
31. Test for Significant Difference between Younger, Middle-Aged, and Older Subgroups' Fixed Sorts and Free Sorts for "Persons between Whom There Is Mutual Social Exchange" 102
32. Test for Significant Difference between Younger, Middle-Aged, and Older Subgroups' Fixed Sorts and Free Sorts for "Higher Statuses" among "Persons between Whom There Is Economic Exchange" 104
33. Test for Significant Difference between Younger, Middle-Aged, and Older Subgroups' Fixed Sorts and Free Sorts for "Lower Statuses" among "Persons between Whom There Is Economic Exchange" 106
34. Test for Significant Difference between Younger, Middle-Aged, and Older Subgroups' Fixed Sorts and Free Sorts for "Higher Statuses" among "Persons between Whom There Is Political Exchange" 108

35. Test for Significant Difference between Younger, Middle-Aged, and Older Subgroups' Fixed Sorts and Free Sorts for "Lower Statuses" among "Persons between Whom There Is Political Exchange" 110

LIST OF MAPS

1. Map of Lebanon, showing location of Barouk . . . . Facing Page 1

2. Map of the village of Barouk, indicating residential locations of the different population subgroups 175

LIST OF PLATES

1. A friend standing before the neighboring village of Fraydis

2. A young man standing before the pine and cedar groves

3. A summertime wedding procession through the market

4. Making *'araq*

5. Druze *'ajawīd* ladies walking through the market in early morning

ACKNOWLEDGMENTS

I wish to thank the Center for Near Eastern and North African Studies and its Director, Dr. William D. Schorger, for supporting the publication of this monograph, which is mainly an ethnography but which also makes some theoretical and methodological points.

The study was originally prepared and submitted in partial fulfillment of the requirements for the degree of doctor of philosophy to the Department of Anthropology at Yale University in 1975. Some of the original analysis has been changed and several parts of the manuscript have been rewritten. The Campus Grants committee of The University of Michigan–Dearborn generously funded the necessary retyping. The comments of Barbara Goldman were especially helpful in pointing out a problem; the aid of Thomas Snabb and Stephen Huxley was important in solving it. My appreciation goes to them, as well as to Victor Ayoub, Leila Barbir, Lars Björn, Robbins Burling, Clement Henry, Suad Joseph, Paul Kabler, Christine Miller, Daniel Moerman, and Martha Morris.

The field research on which the study is based was done in the Lebanese village of Barouk between November 1973 and February 1975. Funding for the research was partially provided by Yale University, and the U.S. Public Health Service partially supported the analysis and writing stages of the dissertation. I am grateful for the help provided by Dr. Harold W. Scheffler, my advisor during this period.

In Lebanon my debts are many. I appreciate the aid which my ex-wife, May Majdalani (and her father, Joseph Majdalani, and brother-in-law, Victor Azar) furnished at key points in the research. At the American University of Beirut, I would like to thank Drs. Samir Khalaf and Fu'ad Khuri for their help and informed comment; Dr. Edwin Prothro and Vice-President Georges Hakim for their support to the research project; and the faculty, staff, and students of the Department of Sociology and Anthropology for their interest and constructive criticism. My appreciation goes also to the members of CEMAM at the Université de Saint Joseph and to officials in the Lebanese Ministeries of Planning, Urbanism, and Interior, as well as in the Geographic Section of the Lebanese army. To the "family of the village" of Barouk,

I offer my gratitude for their hospitality and cooperation: more than by water, climate, or trees, Barouk is "blessed" by its people. My special thanks to to the family of Sheik Kacem al-Emad for their generosity and support; to *ḵawāja* Fawzi and *sitt* Nazik for their kind assistance; and to *sitt* Mantaha, Abu Georges, Abu Jawdat, Abu Jihad, Abu Kimal, and Abu Yusif for their help and affection. Hereafter in this volume all Arabic names of persons have been changed, but I am sure that those concerned will recognize themselves should they ever read this study.

Finally, I would like to make a more solemn acknowledgment. This monograph is dedicated to the memory of Sheik Kacem *bayk* Tamar al-Emad and to the others of Barouk and Lebanon who died in the civil war, 13 April 1975 to 18 November 1976. *'Allah yirhamhom.*

WĀSIṬA IN A LEBANESE CONEXT

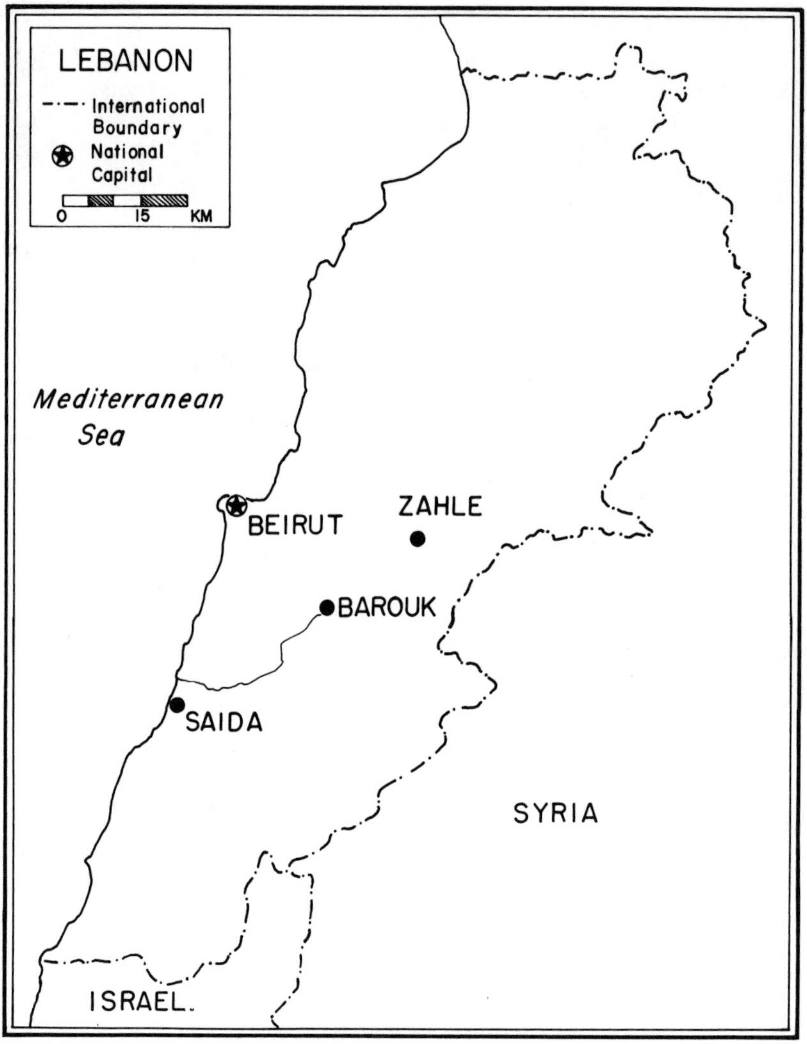

Map of Lebanon, showing location of Barouk

I

INTRODUCTION AND THEORETICAL BACKGROUND

Lebanon is a small country in the Levant, lying between 33° and 35° north latitude (as does South Carolina) and bounded on the north and east by Syria, on the south by Israel, and on the west by the Mediterranean Sea (see Map 1). The country has a population of approximately three million and an area of about 3600 square miles, giving it nearly the same population as Connecticut in a space three-fourths as large. The terrain of the country can be divided into four roughly north-to-south bands: first, a very fertile but narrow coastal plain ("The Sahel"), which is the location of the major cities; second, a mountain range ("The Mountain" or "Mount Lebanon"), which rises above 10,000 feet in some places only a few miles from the coast; third, a fairly level interior valley ("The Biqā'"), which is the northern extension of a rift that continues down the Jordan River Valley and beyond; and finally, a second and generally lower range of mountains ("The Anti-Lebanon"), which parallels the first one.

This geographic context has been an important factor in the historical development of Lebanon. Because the mountains are composed of alternating layers of permeable and nonpermeable rock (Fisher 1971:400), water absorbed by the crests is forced to the surface along lines of juncture between the two strata. At lower elevations the softer rock has eroded faster, so deep ravines and steep cliffs separate the mountain uplands from the coast. Accordingly, water and soil in quantities sufficient to support small populations are present in places which also can be easily defended by their inhabitants.

Consequently, the mountains of Lebanon historically have offered refuge to persecuted minorities in the Levant. Maronite Chirstians, for example, have tended to concentrate in northern Mount Lebanon. Druzes have occupied the middle part of the same area, while Shi'ites have predominated in the southernmost portion of the range. These are only rough approximations, of course, since even within these areas there are villages where the predominating religions differ from the ones surrounding, and there are numerous cases where villages themselves are composed of different sects.

One of the most significant consequences of this distribution of religious sects on Mount Lebanon was the growth of what Rondot calls the "Islamic-Christian symbiosis:"

> It is necessary to signal the progressive development of the Lebanese national personality at the heart of these populations of diverse origins who, from the dawn of medieval times until the beginning of the nineteenth century, affirm and when necessary defend their *de facto* autonomy from the Byzantines, then the Arabs, the Mamuluks, and finally the Ottomans; these mountain people were structured into tribal and pseudo-feudal groups that from the sixteenth century onward were dominated and mediated by two successive dynasties, themselves vassals of the [Ottoman] Porte but largely autonomous in fact. [Rondot 1954: 81][1]

Thus, Lebanon's history of cultural diversity and political autonomy was a major factor affecting the events of the nineteenth century:

> After the suppression of feudalism by the [Shihabi] Princes, then the destruction of the princely dynasty in 1840 by the Porte and its allies, finally from 1840 to 1860 an Ottoman attempt to take matters directly in hand, the socio-political structure of Lebanon is dominated by a major trait: the secular symbiosis of different communities, groups of populations belonging to diverse Christian and Muslim sects defined by their religious affiliations and led by ecclesiastical chiefs whose political importance became apparent thereafter. The Ottomans try to found their power on the destruction of that accord; after the bloody troubles and an intervention by Western powers (1860), Lebanon receives the status of autonomous province, founded especially on the proportional division of powers and public responsibilities among the communities. Liberated in 1918 by the Ottoman defeat, Lebanon makes itself a separate state on this communal basis, regarding which the territorial enlargement in 1920 will diversify and complicate the givens. . . . [Rondot 1954:81]

As Rondot indicates, the Ottoman province of Mount Lebanon served as a model for the state formed in 1920 by the French Mandate authorities. That province had organized the traditional cooperation—or at least mutual tolerance—between the different sects living in the mountains into political institutions: a governor (usually a non-Lebanese Christian) appointed by the Ottomans and a council of representatives appointed by the local religious communities. The "complications" referred to above, however, stemmed from a salient difference between the "Little Lebanon" of the Ottoman province and the "Greater Lebanon" which resulted from including the coastal plain, the interior valley, and the Anti-Lebanon into the new state:

> In the old Little Lebanon, the numerical preponderance of Christians, and even of the Maronites alone (respectively 329,482 and 242,308 of 414,800 inhabitants

[1] Translation of this passage, and all further translations, were made by myself, unless otherwise noted.

in 1913) allowed the drawing of clear majorities, possible bases of government, from the system of proportional representation: it will no longer be the same in Greater Lebanon where . . . no community will hold the majority and the number of Christians will be equivalent to that of Muslims, in practice. [Rondot 1954:84]

Actually the borders of the new state did maintain a tiny Christian majority–something on the order of three percent. Rondot and at least one other scholar (De Vaumas 1955:577) tend to emphasize the economic and historical reasons for the enlargement:

Greater Lebanon: that is to say, the historical Lebanon realized in the sixteenth century by Prince Fak̲r 'ad-Din Ma'an, with ports (Beirut, Tripoli, Saida), sources of grain (the 'Akkār plain, the Biqā'), [had] all sorts of resources. . . . Lebanon was thus rendered viable but its internal equilibrium was modified; this new difficulty doesn't seem, moreover, to have very much preoccupied at first the creators of Greater Lebanon, [who were] particularly sensitive to economic and geographic realities. [Rondot 1954:84]

Other scholars have taken a more jaundiced view of the action by Mandate authorities. Kirk (1964:164), for instance, classified it as "an unashamed policy of 'divide and rule'" and details its consequences in the following manner:

In 1920 the old sanjaq of Lebanon was expanded to three times its size by the inclusion of the predominately Muslim towns of Beirut, Tripoli, and Saida (Sidon); South Lebanon down to the Palestine border, with a predominately Shi'a population; and the fertile Biqā', with a mixed population consisting mainly of Muslims and Orthodox Christians. In this enlarged Lebanon the Maronites and Christians of all sects constituted only a precarious majority. This weakening of the Christian position was perhaps designed to make them more dependent on French protection and less inclined to follow a nationalist line on their own. [Kirk 1964:164]

Whatever the motivations behind setting the new boundaries, Lebanon stopped being an essentially Christian society to become a multi-sectarian one without a definite confessional majority. This established the major framework for the present situation of the country. In addition to the sects already mentioned, Lebanon today includes a fairly large number of Greek Catholics and tiny minorities of Roman Catholics, Jacobites, Jews, Protestants, etc. (There are seventeen officially recognized sects.) Also, following Turkish repression in the First World War and later, significant ethnic minorities of Armenians (divided into at least two religious sects of their own) and Kurds (mostly Sunni) moved to Lebanon. Finally, some 300,000 refugees fled to areas in and around the major Lebanese cities during the fighting in Palestine in 1947-48.

Although there is today a swell of rural immigrants looking for work and fast living in the cities, and a reverse migration to the more clement climate of the mountains in the summer, the geographic distribution of the various religious and ethnic groups has been generally maintained. Thus, the Maronites and Druzes still predominate on Mount Lebanon; the Shi'a, on southernmost Mount Lebanon and in the Biqā'; the Sunni and Greek Orthodox, on the plains and especially in the cities; and the smaller minorities live almost entirely in the cities.

Alongside these differences in geography, religion, and ethnicity, a student of Lebanese society will find others based on politics and socio-economic classes. Given all these differences, it is difficult to make accurate generalizations which are applicable to the whole country. Scholars, therefore, have tended to focus on selected aspects of Lebanon's "plural society," according to their inclinations and specializations. For example, *Politics in Lebanon* (Binder 1966) provides comment by economists, political scientists, historians, newspaper reporters, government officials, and an anthropologist, but even the closing essay is unable to integrate these often interesting, but very uneven, articles into a clear and coherent picture of Lebanese society. Michael Hudson's *The Precarious Republic* (Hudson 1968) does provide such a picture through detailed statistics and insightful analysis, but the account is strongly influenced by the conditions of the Shihabi period and confined to the macro level of analysis. On the other hand, anthropological accounts such as Gulick (1955), Williams (1965), Sweet (1967), and Rothenberger (1970) have tended to present "their" communities of study as independent microcosms, hermetically sealed from outside influence.[2] To my knowledge, no one has yet made a study which would account for phenomena from the micro to the macro levels of Lebanese society.

One way in which this might be attempted is by focusing on processes that operate on, and between, these levels in economic, political, and social contexts. A process which seems to fit these criteria is one the Lebanese call *wāsiṭa:*[3]

> The term *wastah* is colloquial Arabic for an "intermediary," a go-between, or the process of employing an intermediary or go-between, "a process of mediation" in almost any and all types of activity. The *wastah* system is generalized in the society and performs important functions within the family and clan as well as outside it. One needs a *wastah* in order not to be cheated in the market place, in locating and acquiring a job, in resolving conflict and legal litigation, in winning a court decision, in speeding governmental action, and in establishing and maintaining political influence, bureaucratic procedures, in finding a bride, and, in fact, for the social scientist to locate and convince respondents to give an interview. The *wastah* procedure is complex, its rules varied depending on the sphere

---

[2] More realistic approaches are found in Zecher (1967) and Peters (1972).

[3] All transliterations from Arabic will employ the symbols proposed in Wehr (1961), except in cases where another spelling has become standardized (as with place names like Barouk).

> and nature of activity, whether it is legal, familial, economic, etc. [Farsoun 1970:269-70]

A start has already been made in this direction of study by anthropologists Victor Ayoub (1955, 1965, 1966) and Laura Nader (1965*a*, 1965*b*).[4] The present discussion will concentrate on what they have to say about the process of wāsiṭa and specify some of the problems which they raise.

One of the best ethnographic accounts of a Lebanese village is furnished by Ayoub's studies of the mainly Druze locality of "Kallorwan" (Ayoub 1955, 1965, 1966). The detail and clarity of these studies set a high standard of comparison for other ethnographers. Ayoub's original work (1955) focused on the political organization of the village; it dealt with the wāsiṭa process mainly as a way of illustrating how, at many levels, the kin-based political structure of the village interpenetrated and generally dominated the territorially-based political structure of the nation in which it was encapsulated. The two later articles focused on wāsiṭa as the major process of conflict resolution in the village.

Perhaps the best way to begin describing Ayoub's view is to present his description of the usage of the term wāsiṭa:

> The root meaning, I believe, connotes middle or mediate. I observed the use of the term in several contexts. In addition to indicating the activity of mediation, it was also used to denote the group of men who at any time acted as mediators in a dispute. These uses are central to the discussion. However, it was also frequently applied to the act of interceding on behalf of someone, and to the actor behaving as an intermediary, as when a third party represents the interests of a man proposing marriage or seeking relief from harassment by a government agency. It is legend, of course, that in the Middle East one does not do for oneself what might better be done by a friend or a friend's friend. There is yet another use to which the term was put while carrying the connotation of "intermediary." A young lady explained to my wife that there was no *wasta* between herself and her husband to convey the idea that they made no use of contraception. More significantly, in terms of the present discussion, I heard it used in the special context of relieving an ailment, as when a young woman informed me that her doctor had given her a *wasta* for an organic complaint she had. I cannot say that this last connotation of a remedy is the historically more generic significance of the term, but it seems to be logically so for the purpose of mediation in this setting. The mediators want to conciliate, not to judge. The result is compromise, mutual concessions, which leaves each disputant willing to reaffirm the legitimacy of their association with one another. [Ayoub 1966:109-10]

Ayoub has been quoted at length to specify his conception of the usage of the term. Certain aspects of that conception seem questionable—particularly the stress on wāsiṭa as a means for reestablishing prior relations which have fallen into dispute, rather than as a means for establishing new relations. However, Ayoub's conception will be accepted temporarily to

---

[4] Related writings of interest are Farsoun (1972), Gubser (1973), Hottinger (1961, 1966), Khalaf (1968, 1974), Khuri (1969, 1974), Kisrwani (1971), and Samaha (1974).

examine his description of how the process is linked to kinship structure and operates to resolve disputes within that structure.

In Kallorwan the Druzes are organized into two major patrilineal descent groups. These groups, which Ayoub calls "clans" (1966:113), are subdivided into hierarchically ordered subgroups of lesser and lesser inclusiveness as one proceeds "down" from the clan level to the level of individual households (see Fig. 1). Thus, each *'ayli* is composed of *jubūb*; each *jibb*, of *'ahāli 'al-lazim*; and each *'ahl 'al-lazim*, of *buyūt* (Ar. singular *bayt*).[5]

Figure 1
Segmentary Kinship Organization

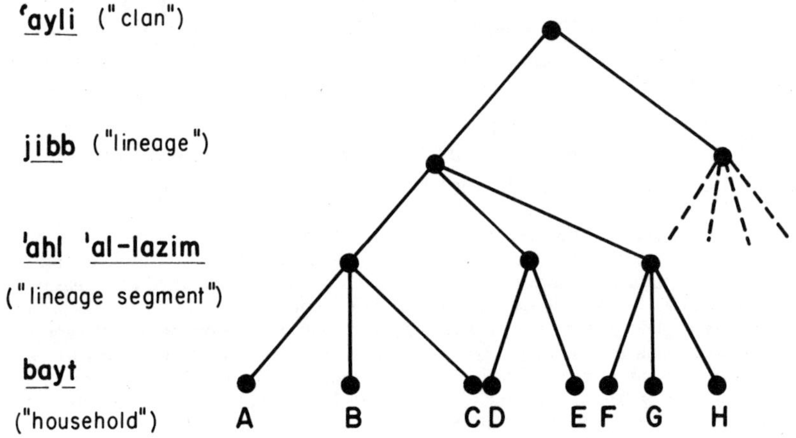

The wāsiṭa process, then, operates to resolve disputes between clan members according to two principles.[6] First is the principle of group unity: every member should support his closest kinsman in a dispute, regardless of the justice of the kinsman's claim. This leaves the problem of whom to support when one is the same genealogical "distance" from all disputants, which is resolved by the principle of neutrality. According to this second principle, every kinsman who is equidistant genealogically from the disputing parties should be neutral. On Figure 1, for instance, if a member of household A has a dispute with a member of household B, households C through H should be neutral. (Of course, all of household A should support their member, and all of household B theirs, according to the first principle.)

[5]See Ayoub (1955:46-79), (1965:140-42), (1966:114-19) for more detailed discussion of these groups.

[6]Ayoub calls these principles "locus of unity" and "equality of social distance" (1966:118).

A dispute with wider implications results if a member of household A is opposed to a member of household H. Then members of B and C should support A; members of F and G, H; and members of D and E should be neutral. A further implication of the principle of group unity is that the "closest neutral" generally should act as mediator and "make the wāsiṭa" between the disputing parties. Thus, to take the first example again, in a dispute between parties from A and B, a member of C will probably provide the mediation because it is the "closest" household in the genealogy.

The two clans in Ayoub's village were each affiliated with clans in other villages on similar segmentary principles, thus leading to the grouping of most Druze clans in Lebanon into two national-level factions[7] called the Yazbakis and the Junblāṭṭis. (More will be said about these factions in later sections.) According to Ayoub's analysis, then, an *inter*clan dispute which is also *intra*factional (i.e., between clans residing in different villages but belonging to the same faction) can be settled by wāsiṭa because both principles—group unity and neutrality—hold. However, in interclan-interfactional disputes, as well as in interreligious or interethnic ones, either the condition of group unity, or that of neutrality, or both, cannot be met. For example, in an interclan-interfactional conflict (i.e., one in which the contending parties belong to different clans *and* to different factions), no Druze could be neutral because there are supposedly only two factions which partition the entire Druze sect. If a Christian were asked to mediate, he would be neutral but lack a structure of group unity to link him to the disputants. Similar considerations apply in the case of interreligious or interethnic disputes. Thus, Ayoub's conclusion follows from his definition of wāsiṭa and the conditions necessary for its operation.

Although his argument is logical, it seems overly restrictive. Ayoub himself mentions an apparent counterexample:

> . . . In 1932 a shooting incident almost precipitated a battle between Druze clans within the village. There is a history of periodic armed conflict between them prior to 1932. At the time, men of Jumblatti and Yazbaki clans from neighboring villages were prepared to converge upon Kallorwan in support of their factional compatriots. As I was told, on each side wiser heads prevailed upon their own hotbloods to control themselves, and then these same men came together to conciliate. Serious trouble was avoided. These proceedings were also classed as *wasta*. I shall disclaim them as such. The conditions of mediation were not met. [Ayoub 1966:117]

It is obvious that the mediators on this occasion were not "neutral," i.e., equidistant genealogically from both parties to the conflict. Nevertheless, armed conflict was avoided and conciliation did occur. A process similar

---

[7]The term *faction* is employed here and throughout this monograph with the senses proposed by Nicholas (1965:44-45). See also the *Conclusion* of this monograph.

to what Ayoub defines as mediation took place under different conditions. Why? He believes that the answer is as follows:

> By 1932, the internal security operations of Lebanon were well established in the Matn [the district where Kallorwan is located]. If armed conflict between the clans had taken place, the gendarmes eventually would have resolved the situation in a manner unattractive to both groups, regardless of their differences. In the Biqā', where even today internal security has not yet been adequately established, interclan quarrels can quickly touch off armed conflict. I would hazard to say that mediators do not so easily and quickly arise. [Ayoub 1966: 118-19]

The answer is not so simple as that. First, a careful analysis of the incident of 1932 can provide some additional insights into the concept of wāsiṭa and how it works. Second, Ayoub's prediction about groups in the Biqā' is hazardous indeed: mediators do operate there under conditions much like those found in Kallorwan (see below).

One salient difference between intraclan mediation and "mediation" in the 1932 incident concerns the number of mediators: in the first case, one group of mediators functions between the disputants at a time; in the second, two groups of mediators functioned simultaneously. Each of these groups first got control of its own clan; then it met with the other to resolve the differences between the two. Furthermore, the common ground between the two groups of mediators was a mutual desire to keep the gendarmerie out of clan affairs. Thus, the potential intrusion of a national political institution prodded the clans into developing a kind of "unity" which they had lacked earlier.

Before drawing out the implications of this incident more fully, let us now deal with Ayoub's prediction about groups in the Biqā'. Laura Nader has written two articles (1965*a*, 1965*b*) about wasita which, although not as detailed nor as explicit as Ayoub's work, do provide interesting similarities and contrasts with it. Nader studied "Libaya," a Shi'a Muslim village of approximately 1400 people in the southern Biqā' valley. The inhabitants of Libaya recognize ten lineage groups within the community. Members of these lineages do not reside together but tend, rather, to be scattered around the village. More important, however, is the way these lineage groups combine into two competing factions:

> Libaya is a village which for as long as anyone can remember has been split into two opposing factions based on family alliances—one headed by the Akls, and the other by the Abrahams. Each faction (except for the rare marriage by capture) is endogamous. The balance of power between factions shifts from time to time, according to one informant, because one or two of the smaller families, described as being peripheral, may ally themselves one way or the other. All the recreative as well as political activities and family or life-cycle activities are patterned along lines of this dual division. No one from the Abraham group attends funerals, weddings, or participates in the men's winter discussion groups with the members of the Akl group or vice-versa. [Nader 1965*a*:395]

Procedures for settling disputes are correlated with this organization of the village into opposing groups. If a dispute occurs between two parties in the same faction, it is generally mediated by older members of their families, or by *'awādim*—"respected individuals who may be from the same half [i.e., faction] or from nearby Shi'a towns." However, if the conflict is between parties belonging to different factions, or between a member of the village and an outsider, the settlement procedure is different. Then the dispute is generally taken to the court of the governmental district in which Libaya is located, and a different kind of intermediary is used (Nader 1965*a*: 395-96).

Even the local representatives of national political institutions conform to this dual organization of the village population. For instance, Libaya has a *mukṯār* ("notary") elected from among the village residents in accordance with national statutes. However, since he is a "son of the village," the mukṯār is necessarily a member of one faction or the other. Although he may mediate disputes within his own faction, he is considered too "biased" to perform this function in interfactional disputes (Nader 1965*a*: 395).

In short, Nader's description of the social organization in the Shi'a village of Libaya is similar in many ways to Ayoub's description of that in the mainly Druze village of Kallorwan. Furthermore, both ethnographers agree that the procedures for settling disputes are correlated with the social structure of the villages where they operate. However, they disagree about the use of mediation to settle interfactional disputes: Ayoub claims that wāsiṭa, as he defined it, cannot function there; Nader says that a kind of wāsiṭa does operate there (and, by implication, in interreligious or interethnic disputes) as well.

Basing her argument on four court cases, Nader tries to show that a kind of mediation has grown out of the contact between national political institutions and village social organization. When a dispute—be it between factions or between a villager and an outsider—is taken to court, each litigant appeals to a professional who can influence the judicial decision in his favor:

> The professional *wasta*-maker . . . does not judge a case. Rather, he uses his persuasive qualities either to effect a compromise or, if the case reaches the court, to swing the decision of the judge in the favor of his man. The man seeking a settlement searches for a *wasta*-maker who has the ability to use language persuasively and has personal contacts at the court where the grievance must ultimately be heard. . . . Furthermore, if the villager in trouble is to find the right *wasta*-maker, he must have acquired a most detailed knowledge of interpersonal relations among the politico-elite in Lebanon. In a sense, the litigant who is the best ethnographer has not only the best chance of winning a case, but in some situations he will be able to influence whether indeed he is to be the plaintiff or the defendant. [Nader 1965*b*:23]

Notice that the procedure involving a professional wāsiṭa-maker and the courts replicates several features of the 1932 interclan incident reported by Ayoub. Again there are two mediating parties, one for each disputant. Again national political institutions foster a kind of unity among litigants, causing them either to compromise or to accept a judicial decision which is likely to be costly for all parties. Finally, Nader's informants classed the use of a professional intermediary and the courts as an example of wāsiṭa, just as Ayoub's informants did with the settlement of the 1932 incident. Neither of these situations, however, fully meets Ayoub's criteria for the proper use of the term.

One must then reexamine those criteria. Ayoub's report on the usage of the term wāsiṭa was discussed earlier in this section. He emphasized the "remedy" sense of the term and apparently slighted other significant aspects of its meaning–in particular, the use of wāsiṭa to establish new relationships. Now it has been shown that Ayoub's account does not fit several cases where social relationships are "remedied" and/or reestablished. Of course, Ayoub can confine his analysis so that it will apply to "intraclan processes only" (1966:108), but doing so causes him to deny important data (intuitions of informants, similarities between intra- and interfactional dispute settlements) and to miss important insights, insights which could lead to a more comprehensive account of organization on both micro and macro levels of Lebanese society.

This critique can be supported by an example from my own field work, whose presentation now is somewhat out of the proper order of exposition but nevertheless is germane to the point under consideration. An incident took place once between three men from Barouk. One of these men was Faruq, an elderly man from one of the "better" families who nevertheless was himself impoverished, uneducated, and living alone in the village. The second was Yusif, a close relative of Faruq but his opposite in almost every other way. Affluent, educated, married into the other "better" family in the village, with children and a high post in the national government, Yusif was at the crown of his life. The third was Abu Karim, an elderly ex-peasant who worked as the caretaker for Yusif's land. A dispute had occurred at some time earlier between Faruq and Abu Karim. Villagers often joked about Faruq behind his back because he expected others to treat him as a sheik while in fact he was old, poor, and without influence. One day as Faruq was out for a stroll, Abu Karim's grandchildren saw him and began mimicking his walk, calling after him, and generally being disrespectful. This blatant effrontery from the grandchildren of a former peasant, the caretaker of his relative, must have cut Faruq deeply. The next time he saw Abu Karim, he denounced the children's manners and the parents and grandparents who had brought them up so badly. Abu Karim lost his temper in return and had to be restrained by others from beating Faruq with his walking stick. From that time on, social relations were cut off between the two men. One day when Yusif came up from the coast to check his house and land, he learned that relations were still broken between Faruq and Abu Karim. After Yusif completed his tour and was preparing to leave the village, several men gathered at his car to wish him good-bye. Faruq, Abu Karim, and I were among them. When Yusif shook hands with Faruq, he asked how he was getting along with me and Faruq said "fine." Then Yusif asked how he was getting along with Abu Karim; Faruq averted his eyes and didn't answer. Yusif looked at Abu Karim and said, "Well, Kimal?" (using Abu Karim's first name instead of the more informal "father of Karim" teknonym generally employed to address or refer to fellow villagers).

Abu Karim moved over, took Faruq's hand and kissed his cheek, saying, "It's finished, Faruq."

Faruq pulled his hand back, turned his cheek, and said "agh!"

Yusif said, "Oh, Faruq," and sighed.

"Why are you trying to mediate between us?" (Ar. *layš ʿam bitjarrib titwassuṭ baynatna*) demanded Faruq. "You have no right to enter." (Ar. *mā ʾilak haqq tidak̲al*).

Yusif sighed again, shook hands with the others standing there, then got in his car and was driven away. I invited everyone present to coffee; Faruq refused but Abu Karim and a couple of other men came along. When we got inside the house, the other men told Abu Karim that he had done the right thing, even though it turned out badly. He replied, "I only did it for the sake of Yusif *bayk*; I can't stand Faruq." Then we had coffee and talked of other things. By the time I left the village in 1975, Faruq and Abu Karim had still not reestablished relations.

Was Yusif's action an example of wāsiṭa? According to Ayoub, it was not.[8] According to Faruq, it was at least an attempted wāsiṭa, as is shown by his use of the verb tawassaṭa to refer to the action. According to me (and, judging from their statements quoted earlier, to Farsoun and Nader also), it was an example of wāsiṭa. If this is correct, then wāsiṭa can operate not only through kinship relations but also through patron-client ones. In the present case Yusif is Faruq's kinsman; he is the patron of Abu Karim. While Faruq could and did refuse Yusif's action, Abu Karim did not and probably could not do so. Thus, the case indicates that a key index to the kinds of relations involved in any particular wāsiṭa transaction is whether the attempt to resolve the conflict can be refused by one or both disputing parties.

[8]The condition of neutrality was not met. Since all three men are members of the same faction, however, the condition of group unity may have been.

It seems profitable at this point to summarize the main elements of the discussion. The original reason for studying wāsiṭa was that it seems to be a process which operates on and between micro and macro levels of Lebanese society. Work by Ayoub and Nader constitutes a beginning to this study; however, that work also embodies some problems. What is needed is a new theoretical model which would capture their essential insights, avoid their problems, and open up inquiry on aspects of the process which have not yet been studied systematically (such as its relation to patron-client ties).

A transactional model, especially one based on Blau's concepts of social exchange, can provide such benefits. In a series of books and articles (1963, 1964, 1968, 1971), Peter Blau has developed an account of how exchange is initiated, built up, and differentiated; how political authority is generated to regulate this process; and how discontent is developed to oppose it. His general procedure is to analyze the processes operating in direct exchange at the micro level, then to expand and supplement these concepts in order to explain indirect exchange in larger and more complex social systems (Turner 1974:265). In the present discussion of this model, attention will be focused on Blau's more recent work and, where relevant, the concepts proposed in these writings will be contrasted with his earlier ones.

By *exchange* Blau means "voluntary social actions that are contingent on rewarding reactions from others and that cease when these expected reactions are not forthcoming" (1968:454). This definition specifies a conception of exchange which is more restricted than Blau's earlier one (1964:6) in order to rule out actions performed under duress of direct coercion, conscience, or irrational impulse. However, the revised definition still seems too broad. Whereas "exchange" intuitively implied a giving and taking, a trade of something for something else, Blau's definition would consider *as exchange* a situation where one party initiated a transaction but did not get a return and so terminated his initiatory actions. That is, Blau's definition would not distinguish between an offer to exchange and an exchange itself, where the offer was accepted and a reward returned. Thus, in this discussion, a more limited definition of exchange will be employed: *exchange* denotes those voluntary social actions which are performed by a party who both expects and receives a reward in return for those actions. That reward may not be the one he expected—it may even not be a fair return, according to his and/or other people's norms of justice—but he must receive a return for the transaction to be called an exchange. Accordingly, a situation where one neighbor helps another, expecting but never receiving a return for that help, is an *offer* to engage in social exchange. Conversely, politicians trading concessions or colleagues swapping advice are *examples* of social exchange.

With this emendation in mind, it is possible to accept most of Blau's other comments about social exchange. Those comments, as Turner (1974: 266) points out, enable Blau to employ terms like *reward* (as a goal sought in social exchange), *cost* (as the alternative goals voluntarily bypassed or foregone), and *profit* (as rewards minus cost) in a precise and delimited manner which contrasts sharply with that of the proponent of another social exchange theory, George Homans.

As the similarity in terminology implies, social exchange is in some ways analogous to economic exchange. For example, in both cases certain actions with an alter are expected to bring returns. Another similarity is that the principle of marginal utility applies: advice can be worth a lot before a problem is solved; after a solution is reached, however, more and more advice on the same matter will tend to be worth less and less. Blau explains this application of the principle as follows:

> The more a man concentrates on obtaining a given social reward rather than others, the more the significance of the alternatives will impinge on his consciousness, making this reward relatively less significant.[9] [Blau 1968:454]

The major importance of this insight is that it helps to explain how exchange not only can establish certain kinds of relationships but also can generate counter pressures to change those relationships. From an individual's point of view, the relative value of a certain reward decreases as its cost rises, i.e., as the individual feels ever more strongly the desire for alternative rewards. From a social point of view, also, the relative value of a certain reward—say, making the police force happier by allocating a larger percentage of the city budget to it—decreases as alternative rewards compete more strongly for attention—say, making sanitation workers happier by granting them pay parity with the police force. The principle of marginal utility, then, explains the dialectical process by which exchange may act as a constructive, and/or a destructive, force in social relations.

Social and economic exchange also differ in some ways. The two variants might be thought of as polar categories which contrast in the degree to which they exhibit several characteristics. For example, social exchange creates more diffuse future obligations rather than the exact stipulations found in a legal contract or bill of sale. Any attempt to specify obligations growing from social exchange converts a more affective association into a "strictly business" affair.

Second, social exchange requires, and even promotes, trust among participants. In the limiting case of an economic transaction, the responsibilities and rights of all parties are spelled out in a manner enforceable by the courts.

---

[9] Of course, marginal utility can also result from factors other than competing alternatives—e.g., from soil conditions which limit the maximum production possible from a piece of land, no matter how much more labor and capital may be invested in it.

In contrast, returning an invitation to dinner by treating the inviter to a cup of coffee is hardly a matter of jurisprudence. Typically, social exchange first concerns minor matters, with little lost if the expected returns are not forthcoming; later it expands to more and more important matters of potentially greater risk, if previous interactions have produced the expected results. As expectations are fulfilled and participants become willing to trade rewards of progressively greater value, social exchange generates the trust it requires to operate.

Third, the rewards sought in social exchange are less detachable from their sources than are economic goods and services. Taking the support derived from a love relationship as one polar example, and the returns from the sale of some item as the other, Blau claims that most social benefits are intermediate between these two extremes. That is, the rewards of social exchange may have a value outside the particular transaction in which they are involved, yet their value will be modified by the nature and intimacy of the relationship concerned. For instance, advice can be bought from a professional consultant, but the counsel of a close friend may be more highly prized.

One of the most interesting characteristics of social exchange is its capacity to create relationships where the actors involved become either equal, or differentiated, in status. Recalling two classic accounts of exchange in non-Western societies, Blau points out that the Kula Ring established relations among peers in the Trobriand Islands; however, some of the potlach ceremonies created status differences among the Kwakiutl Indians in the northern Pacific (Blau 1968:455). Thus, if the original recipient in a transaction returns a reward equal in value to the benefits he received, as in the Kula Ring, he claims equal status with the original provider of the benefit. On the other hand, when the original recipient returns a reward different in value from the benefits received, as with some potlach ceremonies, he claims a status different from the provider's—a higher one, if his return is greater than the original benefits and a lower one, if it is less.

A claim to different status is likely where one or more exchanging parties controls benefits which his alters deem vital, thus giving him potential power over those alters. This potentiality may be actualized when the following conditions are present:

> First, they [i.e., alters] must not have resources that the benefactor needs, otherwise they can obtain what they want from him in direct exchange. Second, they must not be able to obtain the benefits he has to offer from an alternative source, which would make them independent of him. Third, they must be unable or unwilling to take what they want from him by force. Fourth, they must not undergo a change in values that enables them to do without the benefits they originally needed. If these four conditions are met, they have no choice but to comply with his wishes and submit to his power in order to obtain the needed

> benefits. The four alternatives are assumed to be exhaustive; in their absence, the supply of important services inevitably generates power. [Blau 1968:456]

Thus, a participant in exchange can transfer higher status into greater power by recurrently providing benefits which alters can neither return fully nor do without. Blau calls the process by which this occurs "power social exchange"; he contrasts it with "mutual social exchange" and "economic exchange" in terms of the party having discretion over the return. In "economic exchange" neither the original provider of benefits nor their original recipient has this prerogative, since the exact nature and timing of benefits offered and rewards to be returned are specified when the original transaction occurs. In "mutual social exchange" the nature and timing of the return are decided by the recipient of the original transaction. In "power social exchange" the provider of the original transaction decides:

> Accumulated obligations and unilateral dependence transfer the power of discretion over the return from the debtor to the creditor and transform an exchange relation between peers into a power relation between superior and subordinate. [Blau 1968:456]

The discrimination between "mutual" and "power" social exchange is a simpler and stronger categorization than the one Blau proposed earlier (1964:99-100), because the new criterion accounts not only for the nature but also for the timing of rewards. However, the criterion of who decides about returns may appear insufficient to deal with some examples. For instance, suppose a potential follower visits a local political leader several times without receiving a return visit from him, yet still actively helps the leader in an electoral campaign by persuading relatives and friends to vote for him, putting up his posters, etc. Following the successful campaign, the follower goes to ask the leader for a patronage job. If the leader does not deliver, he will be accused of ingratitude and lose the support which the follower has extended to him. Doesn't this situation turn the tables and make the leader inferior, the follower superior? Isn't the provider of original benefits deciding what return he would like and when he would like it?[10]

While social interaction is full of similar tables turned, especially in male-female interactions, a reconsideration of Blau's concepts resolves the apparent paradox. Although his phrasing sometimes is absolute, the conceptual differences Blau has proposed are relative to each other. In the example above, the services provided by the follower may not be vital to the leader, since he can replace one follower among many relatively easily. To the degree that the follower is able to influence others to back his decisions, the

[10] This "example" was originally suggested by Hillary Callan. It is understandable that such an example was originally thought of by a woman. Figuratively speaking, women have been forced beneath men in most cultures and thus have learned to distinguish clearly between apparent and real superiority.

"follower" becomes a "leader" in his own right. Accordingly, he becomes more important to the leader and has a higher status than other followers. If the follower gains sufficient influence, he may engage in mutual social exchange with his former leader and thus gain equal status and power with him. In time, he may even surpass his leader and thus really turn the tables on him, as myriad examples from history attest.

Power social exchange is subject to another transaction:

> The reactions produced by the norms of justice superimpose a secondary exchange nexus upon the primary one—more or less fairness in the primary exchange is exchanged for more or less social approval—and third parties are often drawn into this secondary exchange. [Blau 1971:63]

The idea of secondary exchange is crucial for Blau's attempt to extend concepts from the micro level to the macro level of analysis, from direct to indirect exchange. Briefly put, the concept attempts to account for the processes by which subordinates and others judge the demands made by superiors in power relationships. If greater rewards go to those who have made greater social investments in time and energy, and if subordinates feel the demands made on them are reasonable when measured against the advantages supplied by superiors, those demands are seen as just and fair. Then a consensus develops which supports and legitimates the status and power of superiors by enforcing their demands as examples of "community" values. Conversely, if those demands are seen as unjust and unfair, then a consensus develops which opposes superiors and may lead to their downfall. Secondary exchange, then, expands the impact of transactions beyond direct social exchange:

> Common standards of fairness and justice, for example, have the result that a person's direct transactions with specific exchange partners also involve him in indirect transactions with other members of the community whose social approval for his fair and just dealings he earns or fails to earn. . . . In short, norms of justice promote indirect exchange transactions with profound repercussions for the social structure. [Blau 1971:68]

Shared values thus are crucially important to the social exchange model because, as Blau indicates, they define what rewards men seek in exchange (1968:457).[11] Values, of course, also partly determine what can be exchanged at all. Furthermore, shared conceptions of designative, as contrasted with evaluative, meaning are necessary to identify which goods, services, and/or other "assets" fit into valued categories. If a particular reward is considered "good," "strong," or "active," a party to social exchange must know which other potential rewards are seen as culturally "similar" or

[11] This discussion does not seek to clarify what is already manifest, to "re-invent the wheel." Rather, it attempts to show how Blau's model can be expanded in a rigorous way to account for phenomena that are not linked obviously to exchange processes.

"synonymous" to it and thus become eligible for valued status. This point will be discussed and illustrated in greater detail in Section 3.

It is possible now to summarize the preceding discussion in a taxonomic diagram which depicts relations based on social exchange between different statuses. Figure 2 indicates that Blau's concepts lead to a clear account of how several sets of relationships can be created by "mutual" and "power" social exchange, and how the latter is subject to a secondary exchange which differentiates "legitimate" from "illegitimate" actions. Thus, a relationship between friends or relatives is characterized by "mutual social exchange," a relationship between a leader and a follower by "legitimate, power social exchange," etc. In this way, Blau's model seems to explain how two very different kinds of relations might be developed from the same process, depending on the kinds and amounts of rewards the different participants employ in exchange and on the evaluative and designative conceptions they bring to it.

Figure 2
Taxonomy of Relationships Based on Social Exchange

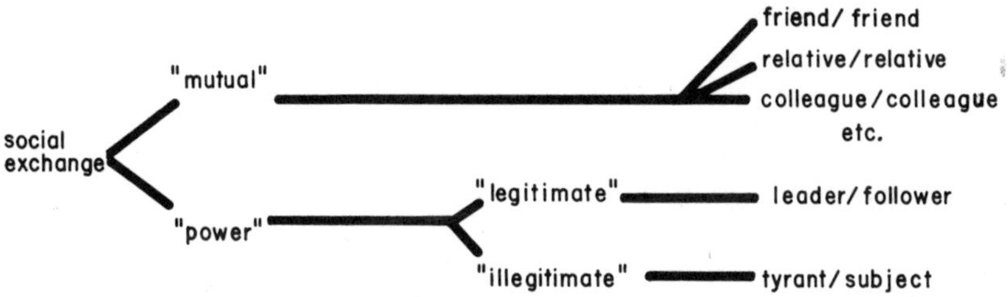

Reconsideration of Yusif's attempted wāsiṭa of the dispute between Faruq and Abu Karim furnishes an illustration of the utility of Blau's model. Yusif is Abu Karim's patron. He employs Abu Karim as the caretaker for his land and has rendered him many services in the past: getting him a second job, taking care of problems he or his family had with the government, etc. Thus, when Yusif indicated that he wanted Abu Karim to take the first step in resolving the dispute with Faruq, he was telling Abu Karim what return he wanted, and when he wanted it, for services rendered in the past and probably to come in the future. Abu Karim, the power subordinate in this relationship, was forced to deliver on demand, if he did not want to be branded ungrateful for past services and/or excluded from receiving future ones. In contrast, Faruq was Yusif's relative. The tie linking these two men is one of kinship: it is buttressed by the social exchange between them, but in their case that tie is not dependent on social exchange. Thus, Yusif can appeal to Faruq on a mutual basis, implying that as a good kinsman he would accept Faruq's mediation in similar circumstances, should the occasion ever arise. Yusif cannot demand that Faruq accede to his wishes, since they are linked as putative "equals." Thus, though Faruq rejected Yusif's offer to mediate the dispute with Abu Karim, he will nonetheless remain Yusif's kinsman and be able to request services from him on the basis of that tie.

While Blau's model thus seems to provide more insight into Yusif's attempt to settle the dispute between Faruq and Abu Karim, the model's overall applicability and ultimate utility can only be measured through more comprehensive study. That is, one must examine exactly how the wāsiṭa process operates in particular ethnographic contexts before one can claim that the social exchange model provides an adequate account of what it is and how it is used. Section 2 will undertake this task for the Lebanese village of Barouk.

II

ETHNOGRAPHY OF FIELD SITE

Barouk (Ar. *barūk*) is located in central Mount Lebanon, 54 kilometers east and a bit south of Beirut. Leaving the capital, the sea road south skirts the shore; then it runs through intensely cultivated plots of vegetables, bananas, and oranges on the coastal plain. Just before the Damour River, the mountain road branches from the coast and follows the river up its path. Passing by a waterfall on the river's major tributary, the road steepens through sinuous switchbacks up a hillside and finally emerges on a shelf high above the river. Following the shelf as it climbs, the road twists through Kfarhim and climbs again. At the head of the slope is Dayr al-Qamar ("the monastery of the moon"), capital of Mount Lebanon under the Ma'an princes and still graced by the sandstone buildings and red-tiled roofs of their period. The road, now a street, turns before a church that once was a mosque, passes the old headquarters where a massacre occurred, and leaves the town as it rounds another curve. Across the valley, the palace of Prince Bashir stretches along a spur, with terraces stepping down all the way to the valley floor. As the road twists around the hill, into gullies and out, angles and perspectives of the palace shift and realign the separate buildings that compose the whole. The road, fairly level now, rounds another corner and the palace is gone. The high chimney and solid stone walls of an old silk-spinning mill come into view, palpable proof of what once was Mount Lebanon's major export. The road then arrives at a junction near the head of the valley. To the right, a road goes back to the Prince's palace; to the left, the road climbs again into the mountains, on the highest ridge of which a dark patch can be seen. Turning left, the road edges up a hill, and valleys open out to the north this time. One can see all the way to the villages along the Damascus highway, 25 kilometers away. The road climbs ever higher and moves through the vineyards and nearly level fields of Kafr Nabraḵ. The dark patch on the mountain is closer now, a deep blue-green against the tan of the slopes below. The road goes through Batloun, turns into another valley.

Barouk is at its head, with the blue-green grove of cedar trees on the mountain directly above. Although the main road goes straight on to the Damascus highway, a smaller one dips down into the valley, crosses a narrow bridge over the trout-clear river, and climbs through fruit trees toward the village. In springtime the trees blossom cherry pink and apple white, with Barouk a cubist jumble of gray stone houses bunched across the hilltop. The road twists sharply around a building, half-house and half-store. The first real houses come into view: the muḵtār's place, Abu Ra'uf's, Sa'id's, the last steep pull past Amin's; then over the hump and into the square. On the right, a short block with stores on either side; on the left, a grocery, a blacksmith, another grocery, and then the road going up to the cedars. Abu Jawdat is sitting on his chair in the sun. Down the street the barber is talking with Abu Riyad. Just an ordinary day, a day like any other in the village.

Barouk is located about 4000 feet above sea level. This altitude makes the climate delightful in summer: warm sun, clean dry air, cool nights, and of course no rain. In the winter the climate is rigorous: rain can continue for days, soaking through the concrete blocks of which many houses are made and putting a damp, soggy pall over everything. In winter, too, the temperature can drop precipitously and the rain pile up as snow. One snowfall reached a meter in eighteen hours at the village, and more than six meters on the top of the mountain near the television tower.

Wintertime moisture, however, sustains Lebanon's largest remaining cedar grove. It also is a key factor in Barouk's sustenence; the rain and snow that seep into the mountain all winter come out rushing and bubbling at the village spring through the long, dry, Mediterranean summer. The village, the trees, the mountain, and the river are all linked, then, and it is fitting that all share the same name.

Villagers give that name different derivations. The most common has it that Barouk is derived from *baraka* ("to kneel, bend") and stems from the period when the flat, wooded area around the spring was a favored stopping-place for the camel caravans carrying grain from Syria to Saida. A second derivation is that Barouk is from *bāraka* ("to bless"), because the area is blessed with abundant water and trees. The least common derivation has it that the name comes from the many "puddles" (Ar. *birak*) where the main spring comes out. Professor Frayha mentions that the name may have come from Hebrew or Phoenician roots, and shows which grammatical models it must follow if it did, but personally he favors the etymology based on "blessing" (Frayha 1956:17).

The "blessed" village, then, was chosen as a research site partly because of its location in the historic heartland of Mount Lebanon. Another reason for that choice was Barouk's sectarian composition: the population, or as they call themselves, the "families of the village" (Ar. *'ahāli 'aḍ-ḍay'a*) can be subdivided into approximately 1500 Druzes, 300 Maronites, and 600 Greek Catholics,[1] totaling some 2400 people[2] during the period when research was done there. Another factor was the apparently wide range of economic differentiation shown by the dress and housing of the villagers. Still another factor was the beauty of the area and the hospitality of Baroukis. But surely one of the most important factors in the choice of this village as research site was an invitation from one of its most influential men to use his house and contacts among the local people.

Those contacts, and the backing implied by offering his house, were valuable assets in establishing a research presence during a period of extreme tension in Lebanon. The latest war between Israel and the Arabs took place in October 1973, just before research was begun. Although Lebanon was not directly involved, the Lebanese of course sided with their "brothers." Economic and medical help was given to the Syrians and news bulletins were followed closely. Fighting actually came closer to Barouk than to many other parts of Lebanon, since the Israelis bombed a radar station near the village during the war. Furthermore, one "son of the village" who had taken Syrian nationality some years earlier and risen to a high rank in the army there disappeared during the war, and members of his family were involved in a six-month effort to learn what had happened to him. Finally, there was frequent aerial combat in the vicinity, and at least two Israeli jets broke the sound barrier over the village, and much of south and central Lebanon, each and every clear day during the period of research. Everyone in the village knew where those jets were made, how they got there, and what my nationality was.

Backing from a local "influential" thus provided an opportunity for working; the trick was learning how to use that opportunity. Since Barouk is divided into two major factions, receiving help from a member of one meant a guarded reserve and little cooperation from members of the other. Nonetheless, it was necessary to accept this handicap in order to work at all. Furthermore, accepting the backing of this particular person made possible a way of dealing with the factional problem, because he is obligated by his job as a government official to live most of the year outside the village. In the summer, however, he sends his family there and joins

---

[1]The last-named sect was formed when a number of congregations split from the Greek Orthodox church in 1709 and recognized the authority of the Pope. Short descriptions of all of these sects and further references on them can be found in Hudson (1968:25-32).

[2]The figure of 2400 was derived by multiplying the average household size times the total number of households registered to vote (7 x 341 = 2387). This figure is approximately one-third of the official estimate of village population. The great discrepancy between estimates can be explained in part by the practice of including persons who have emigrated abroad in the official estimate.

them when he can, on weekends and holidays. Thus, he would need his house for the summer and I necessarily would have to move elsewhere—optimally, among people with whom I had had little contact before.

In the beginning, therefore, almost all interaction was with a small group of villagers: socially, with the clients of my backer and their families; economically, with the merchants—all the merchants, a little from each—in the market. Proceeding in this way allowed working on several basic skills.

First, it provided an opportunity to develop greater fluency in the language spoken in the village. While the Arabic used there is, of course, mutually intelligble with that spoken in Beirut, there were small differences in grammar, vocabulary, and pronunciation. An interesting example of the last is a supposedly sectarian difference: Druzes in Lebanon are said to use the *qaf* (i.e., the significant sound unit written in Arabic by ق) while speaking Colloquial Arabic, but speakers belonging to other sects supposedly replace it with a glottal stop (i.e., the significant sound unit written in Arabic by ء). This generalization is actually too broad on two accounts: first, Druzes who live away from the villages often do not speak with the qaf; and second, in some villages, members of other sects use the qaf as often as their Druze neighbors do. In Barouk, an intermediate situation is found. Those Druzes who live in the village only during the summer generally do not use the qaf; most members of other sects residing in the village also do not use it. Thus, pronunciation patterns in Barouk reflect, to a certain degree, either what a person's residential pattern is or what sect he belongs to.

Second, the restricted interaction characteristic of the beginning of research enabled me to learn how visiting is done in the village. One of the purportedly universal institutions of the Middle East is the coffeehouse, where men—and only men—gather to chat, play games like backgammon or cards, smoke water pipes, etc. The coffeehouse acts as "neutral ground" where a man might meet any other from the village or quarter. Interestingly, though, there are no such coffeehouses in Barouk.[3] The cafes near the spring are open regularly only during the summer and depend on outsiders for their trade. Since many people come to visit the cedars, and the spring is a delightful, cool and shady place in its own right, these cafes do a brisk business, especially on weekends. Two other small cafes near the school and on the road to the cedars also depend on schoolchildren and/or visitors

[3] The absence of coffeehouses may be linked to the sectarian composition of the village. It is plausible (and certainly testable) that coffeehouses are generally found in areas where the population is predominantly Muslim. Coffeehouses offer places where men can meet without entering each other's homes, which traditionally are the domain of women and thus off-limits to males outside the family. Druze and Christian women, in contrast to Muslim women, are accorded higher jural statuses and responsibilities, including more personal responsibility for their own modesty. Accordingly, the spatial separation of sexes is not so rigidly enforced among Druzes and Christians, and coffeehouses are less important to their society.

for their business. Therefore, almost all social life in the village is effected through making or receiving visits in the home. This, of course, is the standard pattern for the social life of women in the Middle East, but in Barouk it is characteristic of both sexes. During the day, men usually visit men and women visit women; at night, men and women together often visit other couples. Interacting intensely with a small number of families, then, afforded the opportunity to learn customary expressions ("I hope you're enjoying yourself here?" "In your presence."), topics of polite conversation (the weather, international politics, differences in styles of life and social customs between America and Lebanon), and the hospitality generally offered to visitors (maté, fruit, coffee, and candy).

An especially interesting aspect of the last is the maté-drinking ritual. Maté comes from South America and the Druze claim their emigrants to that region brought the custom back to Lebanon. Maté is served in a small, hollowed-out gourd. The flakes are first poured into the gourd, filling it approximately half full. Then either hot milk (in the morning) or hot water is poured over the maté. Sugar may be added.[4] Then a metal straw with a screen-like attachment is inserted into the broth inside the gourd. Generally the person making the maté drinks the first one in order to assure that everything is all right; then he or she adds more liquid and passes the gourd to the highest-ranking visitor. If all present are intimates, the gourd goes to the first person on the maker's right. The order of serving is thus indicative of social relations between the persons present. I heard a story several times about how Prince Majid 'Arslān, leader of one of the two traditional factions of the Druzes, was once visiting a village. The villagers began preparing maté for him and he sat down just to the left of the man making it. When the second gourd of maté was ready, the maker passed it to the first man on his right. Others present began criticizing the maker for not presenting the gourd to the guest of honor, but the Prince silenced them by saying that he had been paid an even higher honor.

Games sometimes provided variations to this standard visiting pattern, especially when men visited men. Villagers play two kinds of backgammon, with the more complex kind–*maḥbūsi* ("imprisoned")–generally favored over one much like the American game. Two simpler versions of bridge, *bāsara* and *ṭromb* (or *ṭurnīb*) are also played.

As time went on, I began to perceive other variations in the standard visiting pattern. For instance, I learned how people indirectly asked for

[4]The importance of factions in village life is indicated, among other ways, by the amount of sugar added to coffee or maté. Members of one faction traditionally add a lot and identify the beverage offered to them as, for example, "maté X" (X being the name of the major family in the faction) or "maté not X." Many members of the other faction, in contrast, drink their maté, and sometimes their coffee too, without any sugar at all.

and got information that might be considered sensitive by the speaker. Often this involved making a somewhat exaggerated statement of a person's views on a matter, so that the person concerned would feel obliged to correct and clarify just what his views were: "I'll bet you went to the meeting just to laugh at people"; "No, I went in order to . . . . " Other times it might be done by providing a bit of information about a person and asking for another bit: "The brother of 'Ali who works on the highway crew; whom did he marry?" Also, people began to speak more openly about local events and show aspects of their views on village social life. For instance, people often spoke of *hal-ḥāra* ("this section of the village") and *haddīk 'al-ḥāra* ("that section"). In Barouk, residence tends to be patrilocal and the area where members of a patrilineal descent group generally live comes to be known as their "section."[5] Speaking of a certain "section" then, was an indirect way of referring to a group of people, i.e., the faction, sect or largest family living there. After I thought I had learned what hal-ḥāra meant, the next time I heard the expression I asked, "hal-ḥāra, you mean family X, family Y, and family Z?" (all members of the same faction and sect except for family Z). When the answer was "No, family Z is in haddīk 'al-ḥāra," I felt that I understood the meaning of these expressions.[6] Interestingly, additional corroboration was furnished to this hypothesis some months later, after I had moved from my backer's house, when I visited a villager on the occasion of his daughter's marriage. Several of us were joking with the father of the bride when one of the men jibed that here I had been his neighbor all these months and yet he still didn't know my full name. (Generally, I was called "*k̲awāja 'al-Fred*" or "*'al-'amerikāni.*") One of the other men present said, "He was your neighbor, but now he's living in that section." "Yes," added another, "and that section belongs to Kimal bayk, but this one belongs to Prince Majid," to general laughter and assent. A short while later he added an aside to me personally: "Of course, we're only joking now because the village is united" (*'aḍ-ḍay'a ḍay'a wāḥida*).

A third consequence of restricted interaction early on was the opportunity to learn more about local kinship organization. Terms for both consanguineal and affinal relatives were the same, with one exception, as those discussed by Millicent Ayoub (1957:18-65) in her excellent study

[5]These are only tendencies, for a few households from at least one other family are found in almost every section. See Map 2 for details.

[6]The names of these sections show an interesting pattern of sectarian differences. Whereas the Druze ones are given family names (*ḥārat 'al-X*, "the section of the X family"), Christian ones are given sectarian names (*ḥārat 'al-mawārni*, "the section of the Maronites"). These naming patterns were checked several times with both Druze and Christian informants.

of Druze kinship and marriage. The exception was the term *'ikwi* ("siblings"), which is used mostly in reference but may also be employed in address, to any collection of two or more siblings of either sex.

Groups based on an ideology of patrilineal descent were organized somewhat differently from those described by Victor Ayoub, whose remarks were discussed in Section I of this study. (The reader may wish to consult Fig. 1 in this volume, for a diagram illustrating Ayoub's analysis.) On the one hand, the term 'ahl 'al-lazim was not used in Barouk to denote a level of segmentary structure above that of bayt but below that of jibb: buyūt were grouped into jubūb and jubūb into *'aylāt*. Since one level of segmentation was removed, this difference made descent group organization simpler. On the other hand, the meanings of the terms jibb and 'ayli seemed more complex. Members of a given jibb generally claimed descent from the man for whom the group was named, but they also were unsure about, or gave conflicting accounts of, the exact genealogical links between them. For such a group, then, "clan" seems to be a better English gloss than Ayoub's "lineage" is. A number of such clans were combined into a group called an 'ayli, whose members generally shared a common last name, often resided together in one section of the village, and sometimes formed an officially recognized association (Ar. *rābiṭa 'aylīya*) to promote their common interests. For Barouk data, then, Arabic 'ayli might better be glossed in English by a more general term, such as "family."

Affinal relations in the village seemed to be more complexly structured than the ones in Kallorwan, as described by Millicent Ayoub (ibid.). While most marriages apparently were between members of the same family, there were smaller numbers of marriages within the faction but outside the family, a few outside the family and faction but within the sect, and a very few even outside the sect. Furthermore, it seemed there was a class barrier within the Druze sect, since descendants of the former *mušāyik* ("noble") class were not supposed to marry descendants of the former *'āmmīya* ("commoner") class. The actual situation with regard to both consanguineal and affinal relations turned out to be more complicated than these first impressions indicated, but they did provide important clues to guide further research.

One of the major ways by which that further research became possible beyond the small nucleus of original informants was making visits for what villagers called *wājibāt* ("social obligations"). The most important of these was attending mourning ceremonies. Every adult member of the community is expected to attend every ceremony; if for some reason he cannot, he is expected to pay his respects to the family of the deceased at the earliest possible date afterward. If he does not fulfill that expectation, people will speak critically of him and may boycott ceremonies for his family or even cut all social contact with him. In a literal sense, then, attending such ceremonies and performing the proper rituals of greeting, respect, and leave-taking are the minimal requirements to participation in community life.

Shortly after a person dies, members of his family decide when and where the mourning ceremony will be held and then contact others by messenger (especially in the village), telephone, or letter. If the deceased was a Druze, the mourning ceremony is called an *'azā'*. This ceremony begins early on the appointed date, when close male relatives and friends form a line in an open area, usually the street, near the home of the deceased. There they receive the condolences of people who come to pay their respects. If the deceased was a Christian, the ceremony is called a *jinnāz*, and the reception line is generally formed near the dead person's church. Women of both sects generally receive and pay visits of respect in the home of the deceased. Those paying respect often do so as delegations linked by kinship (e.g., families), common residence (e.g., villages), or mutual interests (e.g., political parties).

In the Druze ceremony, a group of mourners forms by late morning and begins chanting as it moves slowly up and down the street where men pay their respect. Women at the house of the deceased also chant over the open coffin containing the body. At the time chosen for burial, a party of men goes to the house, closes the coffin, and brings it out to the street. There a procession is formed, with the religious specialists (*mušāyiḵ 'ad-dīn*) first,[7] then bearers of flowers, then the coffin, then the family and close friends of the deceased, and finally everyone else. Women do not join this procession, but there may be a band playing dirges just behind the religious specialists. The coffin is carried to an open spot near the family tomb and the mušāyiḵ 'ad-dīn form a circle around it. A few of them are called out, one to chant the "God is greater" prayer and the others to go through the motions associated with it. When the prayer is finished, these men return to the circle and the whole group begins swaying rhythmically right and left and praying for the deceased. At a point during this prayer, the bystanders participate by saying *'allah yirḥamo* ("May God have mercy on him.").[8]

[7] I was told that until the recent past, descendants of the old mušāyiḵ class used to walk in front of the mušāyiḵ 'ad-dīn in this procession. People then began to criticize them for this, so some of them boycotted funerals of the 'āmmīya class. Then members of the 'āmmīya class boycotted mušāyiḵ funerals until a compromise was reached. Today the mušāyiḵ often walk with the close family and friends of the deceased.

[8] A factional difference was pointed out to me in the number of blessings said for the deceased: supposedly members of the Junblāṭṭi faction say one for everyone, while members of the Yazbaki faction say as many as the deceased is felt to merit because of piety, good works, etc. At the mourning ceremonies I attended, the difference was present and seemed to be an example of the way political differences can become reflected in theological practices. Since I left the village, however, other informants have cautioned me not to take the purported difference as a general rule; they also have provided examples where it probably would not apply. Accordingly, final clarification of the matter requires further study.

When the prayer finishes, family or close friends may say a few final words, and a professional poet is often brought in to comment on the life of the deceased and the sad circumstances under which all present were brought together. Some of the final commentaries are moving tributes indeed. Then the coffin is placed in the family tomb, a prayer said at the door, and the tomb closed. Finally, the family and close friends of the deceased form another reception line, and all those present take their leave as they file out, the mušāyik̲ 'ad-dīn leaving first.

For the Christian ceremony, the body is brought to the church and prayers said over it by the religious specialist (*k̲ūrī*). Although either men or women may attend this part of the ceremony, generally most of the participants are women, and men remain in front of the church to receive condolences. When the prayers are finished, a procession is formed to carry the body to the tomb where it will be buried. First in the procession comes the cross-carrier, then bearers of flowers or other banners and pictures, then the priest(s), then the coffin, then the close male relatives and friends of the deceased, and finally everybody else. Again, women do not join the procession, but there may be a band. The coffin is carried to the family tomb, a prayer said, and the door of the tomb closed. Then the family and close friends of the deceased form another reception line, and all those present pass by it to take formal leave as they depart.

As the meaning of the word indicates, an 'azā' is primarily a ceremony of solace and consolation for the loved ones of the deceased. A jinnāz, on the other hand, is a ceremony which prepares the deceased for proper burial. The Druze choice of the term 'azā' to designate their mourning ceremony may well be tied to their belief in *taqammuṣ* ("reincarnation").[9] Since the deceased will be reborn someday as a Druze, the focus of ceremonies should be on those who are left behind, those who are forced to bear the grief of departure. I often heard an analogy which is consistent with this interpretation. Druze people say death and the grief it causes are like a bar of soap: at first it is very big and important, but over time it gets smaller and smaller without anyone paying it particular notice, until one day it's all gone.

Probably the next most important example of visits made for wājibāt is attending weddings. Again, every adult is expected to attend every wedding, but compliance is not so strictly enforced. One particularly forthright young man told me, "I go to their (i.e., my villagers') mourning ceremonies because I want them to come to mine. I don't go to their weddings because I don't care if they come to mine."

---

[9]Probably the most comprehensive study of Druze doctrines and theology in a Western language is De Sacy (1938). See also Bouron (1930), Makarim (1974), Najjar (no date), and Bryer (1975).

These two occasions, mourning ceremonies and weddings, are the polar examples of the category of wājibāt. Expressed more generally as *karih* ("unpleasantness") and *faraḥ* ("happiness"), these poles encompass milder occasions from visiting a sick person or consoling someone who failed an examination, on the one hand, to visiting parents of a new baby or congratulating a person with a new job, on the other. As was explained above, accounts are kept of these visits and the rule of reciprocity holds. A party who has not yet fulfilled the expectation of making such a visit is obliged or *madyūn* ("indebted") to the people expecting it. According to the model of social exchange presented in Section I, then, wājibāt visits act to establish mutual relationships between the different families, factions, sects, and—at least today—classes within the community, as well as to people outside it.

Another category of visits is those made *bidūn taklīf* ("without ceremony, cost"). Included in this category are visits between members of a family or close friends, people who enjoy each other's company very much and are intimate with each other. Accordingly, such people can visit each other at any reasonable time of the day or night, without invitation or formality. Of course, no close accounting (or "cost") of such visits is made and the rule of reciprocity is only loosely applicable. Thus, one party may visit the other many times without receiving a return visit or without even thinking about, let alone reminding the other of, his obligations.

A third category of visits is those made for a *maṣlaḥa* ("particular interest, benefit"). Such visits occur, for example, when a person calls on someone else in order to have a favor arranged, to ask for help or advice, etc. Since these visits are not "repaid" by return visits, superficially they might appear to loosen or drop the rule of reciprocity. Under examination, however, this turns out not to be the case: visits for a maṣlaḥa are recompensed by the attempt to deliver the goods or services requested. If the person visited is successful (i.e., he delivers the goods or services), then an exchange relationship is established between him and his visitor. Accordingly, the original visitor will be required to make a return of some kind at a later date. As was discussed in Section 1, if he cannot return goods and services considered culturally equivalent in value to those he received earlier, then he will take the inferior status in what has become a relationship based on power social exchange.

Surely one of the most common examples of this sort of visiting in Lebanon occurs when supporters call on their *za'īm* ("political leader"):

> Allegiance to the *za'īm* is in peacetime exteriorized by visiting him. He is visited not only when help, intercession, protection, etc., are needed, but also at the "right" time intervals and in the "suitable" fashion (varying with the position of each client) to show that the client still belongs to his party and does want to be at his disposal, just as he expects the *za'īm* to be at his disposal. [Hottinger 1961:129]

One informant from Barouk gave the following general explanation of how such visits take place and what the "right" time intervals and "suitable" fashions are for their occurrence:

> The person seeking help in some matter–say, dealing with the government–visits an important personality to ask for a *wāsiṭa*. Such an important personality would be either someone in the government or with power (Ar. *nufūz*) as if he were there. This *zaʿīm* listens to the person and, if he wants to help him, gives him a card with the *zaʿīm's* name on it. Next the *zaʿīm* contacts, through a visit or a telephone call, the government official who has responsibility for the matter which the person requested. Then the person visits the government official, presents the *zaʿīm's* card, and makes his request. And then the official takes care of the matter for him. Later on, the person goes back to the *zaʿīm* to thank him for his help (Ar. *musāʿdi*) and visits him once or twice a year thereafter. Sometimes the *zaʿīm* later asks for his help. For instance, once they asked my brother and me to go to another village, curse the *zaʿīm's* electoral opponents, tear down their election posters, shoot in the air, and say we were from the X family in Barouk but we were for *zaʿīm* Y. Actually, we support him not because of his politics but because we need services (Ar. *wasayiṭ*, plural of *wāsiṭa*) and because personally he is a fine man. [personal interview]

The relationship between a zaʿīm and his *zilm* or *'atbāʿ* ("supporters") has very deep roots in Lebanese history. During the feudal period, for example, a somewhat similar relationship existed between a *muqatiʿji* or *'iqtāʿi* ("feudal lord," i.e., the *šayk̲* who controlled a feudal district or *'iqtāʿ*) and his *'uhda* ("charges"):

> For a man to be of the *'uhdah* of a *muqatiʿji* involved moral obligations not only on his part but also on that of the lord, who would come to the aid of the subject and protect him. In the language of the period the *muqatiʿji's* responsibility for the subject's welfare was described as "tending and protecting." To maintain his integrity and position in the political life of the *Imarah*, a *muqatiʿji* was well aware that he had to have a strong following and a loyal one. Sometimes, in protecting their followers, *muqatiʿjis* went so far as to place political considerations above accepted rules of good conduct on the part of the subject. [Harik 1968:43]

As Khalaf (1974:7-9) has indicated, this relationship involved "the exchange of support for protection." The 'uhda provided support to the muqatiʿji and, in return, he provided protection to them–a perfect example of a relationship based on power social exchange. Furthermore, this feudal tie often crossed sectarian boundaries:

> The population was of mixed religious affiliation, which did not coincide with social stratification. Both general classes, *muqatiʿjis* and subjects, contained a mixture of Druze and Maronites. The ruling family of Shihab was Sunni Muslim; and although some of the family became converted to the Maronite faith starting in the mid-eighteenth century, the early converts were not in line for succession. The general population was also quite mixed. The great majority were Maronites and Druze, and then came Christians of various other sects, Shiʿis, and Sunnis. Political allegiance was not based on religious or ethnic considerations, and political loyalty cut across sectarian lines. A man's allegiance was first to his *muqatiʿji* and then to the ruling *Amir*, whether they were of his religious group or not. [Harik 1968:42]

Thus, the ties of allegiance within a particular feudal district were "contracted" between commoners and their muqati'ji on the basis of an exchange of reciprocal services. Where the 'iqtā' contained more than one sectarian group, which was usually the case (see Khalaf 1974:14), such ties crossed the sectarian boundaries concerned.

Hottinger has claimed the contrary:

> In Lebanon there seems to have been one precondition for preserving the all-important loyalty of the people (whose status changed gradually from feudal subjects to that of more or less voluntary clients) and this was religion. In order to win and hold the confidence of his client group, the *za'īm* had to be, and still is, of the same religious community as the people over whom he rules or for whom he speaks or takes action. [Hottinger 1966:89]

There are historically attested cases where families have changed their religions; for example, the Sunni Shihabs and the Druze Abi 'al-Lam'as became Maronites, as Hottinger indicates. However, he also cites the Junblaṭṭs and 'Arslāns as examples, basing this citation on the genealogies which those two families claim. Anyone who has studied the ways genealogies are manipulated to express alliances and/or other fluctuating relationships among groups would be far more hesitant to rely on them as statements of historical fact. Furthermore, the functional reason which Hottinger provides to support his claim—"relations of trust can only develop between people belonging to the same religious community" (Hottinger 1966:89)—is contradicted by the historical evidence. Such relations did develop across sectarian lines, as Harik (1968:42-47), Khalaf (1974:5-12) and Touma (1971:77-83) have shown. Considering the situation from the perspective of a social exchange model might help to explain how such relations of trust actually did come to pass. As a muqati'ji and his 'uhda exchanged protection for support over a period of time involving repeated transactions, each one came to know pretty well what to expect from, and consequently how far to trust, the other. Thus, Hottinger's claims about the "precondition" of sectarian identity seem to be mistaken on both historical and functional grounds.

Reciprocal ties based on exchange also seem to have operated at political levels above that of the individual feudal district. In theory, all the muqati'ji families had a say in choosing the 'amīr. In practice, the strongest ones organized the others, and their followers, into two competing factions (the Yazbaki and Junblāṭṭi *ġaraḍīyāt*), each one backing its own candidate for the office of 'amīr and constantly maneuvering for power and influence viz-a-viz the other.[10] When a leader switched allegiance from one faction

---

[10] This account of the establishment of the Yazbaki and Junblāṭṭi factions contrasts with that given by Abu Shaqra. According to him, the factions developed as follows: the Abu Shaqra and 'Abd 'aṣ-Ṣamad families organized the other 'āmmīya families in

to the other, he usually took "his followers" with him. Thus, the common people were most closely affiliated to their feudal leaders, next most closely allied to the factions of which their leaders were members, and finally linked to the 'amīr (Harik 1968:42-47).[11]

One point needs to be emphasized about these relationships based on exchanges of services between different classes, sects, and regions in the feudal period: such relations were usually established between parties representing their families, and not merely themselves.[12] Internally, families were organized on a segmentary model that was patrilineal, patrilocal, and patriarchical. Externally, families were organized into classes, factions, sects, and villages. Just as "a title of nobility applied to all members of a patrilineal kinship group, not to one or a few members only" (Harik 1968:40), so also did the commoner rank of a family attach to all its members. Similarly, "the fidelity to the parties [i.e., factions] was a function of a familial, and not an individual, cleavage" (Touma 1971:79). Since one's family, class, faction, sect, and residence were either completely or in large measure determined at birth, then, the margin of maneuver possessed by any one individual was extremely limited. Of course, a muqati'ji usually had a much wider margin of maneuver than one of his 'uhda because the muqati'ji controlled more, and more varied, assets which he could use as rewards in social exchange. However, even the lowest peasant had some margin of maneuver based on control of his labor, skills, personal contacts, etc. Furthermore, either lord or commoner could augment his influence by acting in concert with his most natural allies—those whose class, sect, faction, and residence were most like his own—his family:

---

several feudal districts into two groups (the *šaqrawīya* and the *ṣamadīya*); 'āmmīya families in two other districts each organized similar groups; then the šaqrawīya allied with one group in each district and the ṣamadīya did so with their opposing groups; and finally šayḵ 'Ali Junblāṭṭ took the šaqrawīya as his supporters, leaving the ṣamadīya to affiliate themselves to the 'Imad family to form the Yazbaki faction (Abu Shaqra 1952: 84-84).

[11] At the risk of indulging in "pseudo-history," some information obtained from field research supports the general argument advanced above. The traditional organization of society into alliances of families across class and sectarian boundaries was manifested at the village level in Barouk, I was told, by the customary ways of handling local affairs. Before 1926, and stretching back as far as anyone had heard of, a "town council" had deliberated and decided local affairs. This council was formed of one šayḵ from each of the two muqati'ji families, one šayḵ 'ad-dīn from each of the two groups of Druze commoner families, and one priest from each of the two Christian sects in town, giving a total membership of six men. The sectarian composition of the council was thus four Druzes and two Christians, and the class divisions were represented by two nobles and four commoners. The factional composition, however, was evenly balanced: since each local faction contained a šayḵ, a šayḵ 'ad-dīn, and a priest, there were three Yazbakis and three Junblāṭṭis on the council.

[12] It is perhaps indicative that only the last and most recent of four contracts from the feudal period which are presented by Polk (1961:60-70) is between two individuals. The others are between families or, in the earliest one, between noble families and the common people residing in two villages.

> Numerous secondary formations, seemingly sub-factions, managed to acquire their own personalities, their own wills, while simultaneously contributing to the power of the principal group and influencing the decisions of the whole in a degree proportional to their force. Families which counted from 100 to 200 men capable of bearing arms existed (they still exist) in the majority of Lebanese regions and they favored the formation of compact groups possessing an almost clan-like solidarity at the same time that they contributed to the reinforcement of the parties[i.e., factions] which succeeded in pulling together most of them. [Touma 1971:79]

Today, of course, relationships based on exchange have multiplied in number and complexity: households of families—or even their individual members—may leave the alliances contracted by kinsman and establish their own links elsewhere, according to what they conceive to be their paramount interests. This general point was illustrated very well by a connected series of incidents which took place in Barouk while research was going on there.

Late one Saturday night we received a visit during a driving rainstorm. The visitor, Abu Fu'ad, was an elderly gentleman who worked for a government ministry as a watchman over the reforestation project on the mountain above the village. Abu Fu'ad seemed very upset and asked almost immediately if he could use the telephone. I said of course he could and dialed the number for him. As he was talking, my ex-wife made coffee; when Abu Fu'ad finished talking and came out, we invited him to have a cup. He drank it hurriedly, in a preoccupied manner. I asked if something was the matter; he said no, it was nothing important. Then he asked if we were going down to Beirut the next day, as it was our custom to spend Sundays with in-laws there. We said we were and invited him to come with us. He asked when we planned to leave and we told him the usual, about 10:00 or 11:00. He said he had to go down earlier, thanked us for the offer, and left.

When I returned to the village on Tuesday, I went to visit another friend. As we were drinking maté, my friend asked if I had heard about Abu Fu'ad. I said that I had been in Beirut, what happened? He answered that another villager had gotten a recommendation to replace Abu Fu'ad as watchman when he retired in July, and now Abu Fu'ad was trying to arrange that the job be given to his son instead. This other villager had many goats and sheep and had to be on the mountain anyway, so he had been taking cheese and yoghurt to the inspectors and technicians in the government ministry to get friendly with them. This year-long policy had finally paid off when they recommended him for Abu Fu'ad's job. Still, added my friend, Abu Fu'ad could get the job for his son if he had a strong wāsiṭa to help him.

When we finished the maté, my friend walked home with me. No sooner had we arrived than along came Abu Fu'ad, wearing his best dark suit and fez. Since I knew those were his clothes for formal visits, I invited him and the other friend in for a cup of coffee. As I began to make it, Abu Fu'ad announced that he had been completely successful in getting the job for his son. Earlier he had been waiting to finish his term before passing the job on, but when the other villager played his cards, Abu Fu'ad had been pushed to move quickly. "You see," he said, "the job is important because it pays twice as much as the municipal government pays its watchmen and, with our land and crops, it will provide enough income to support my son and his family." We said that we understood that but we didn't see how he had been able to change things after the other villager had been recommended by the employees of the ministry. "I got a stronger wāsiṭa," he said. Since the other villager was a member of local family X, which almost always supports a well-known zaʿīm, Abu Fu'ad went to that very zaʿīm's office for help. Although he comes from local family Y, which is part of the faction traditionally opposed to that zaʿīm, Abu Fu'ad had personally begun supporting him long ago. During the *ṯawra* (Ar. "revolution"–i.e., the unrest that took place in 1958), he was the only member of his family to support the zaʿīm and he even led a group of "revolutionary troops" because he had had military experience. Accordingly, Abu Fu'ad was known to be a friend when he went to the zaʿīm's office in Beirut early Tuesday morning. The secretary there recorded his name, address, and the service he desired on a list which was presented to the zaʿīm. There were many people at the office to request services, so only five or six were admitted at a time, according to the order of the list, into the inner office. There the zaʿīm was sitting at a table, with two assistants nearby calling on the telephone. The zaʿīm read through the list to see what service was desired–be it finding work, getting a promotion, arranging for a license or permit, etc.–and then he told the visitor whether or not he could deliver that service. In Abu Fu'ad's case, he could. As Abu Fu'ad recounted the story, the zaʿīm telephoned directly to the minister of the governmental bureau concerned, identified himself, and said "our friend (Ar. *ṣāḥibnā*) Abu Fu'ad has been doing a good job as watchman for the reforestry project in Barouk. Now he wants to retire and put his son in his place." The minister replied, "at your service" (Ar. *ʿumrak*). So the zaʿīm told Abu Fu'ad that everything would be taken care of when he went to the minister's office. Abu Fu'ad went directly there, was received by an assistant of the minister, and invited into the assistant's office. There his name was checked; then the assistant promised that Abu Fu'ad's son would get the job as soon as formal application procedures were completed and Abu Fu'ad had retired. The assistant also gave his telephone number to Abu Fu'ad so that he could call, after the formalities were completed, to take down the number of the official declaration naming his son to the post.

I asked how Abu Fu'ad was sure that the other villager would not go now to the same zaʿīm and ask him to change the decision; after all, the villager's family were strong supporters of that zaʿīm and he wouldn't want to weaken that support. "Not him," said Abu Fu'ad. "Everybody knows that once he gives his word he doesn't go back on it for anybody, or anything. If he says he will help you, that's it. Because of that, and the fact that he doesn't take money from the government or the people he helps, people trust and support him." Abu Fu'ad then explained that he had expressly chosen to ask for this zaʿīm's wāsiṭa in order to head off any attempt by the other villager to mobilize traditional alliances of support: "I cut the grass from under his feet" (Ar. *qataʿt 'al-ḥašīš min taḥt 'ijray*).

Later, when an inspector from the ministry came to Barouk in order to examine the reforestry project, he went to see Abu Fu'ad. The local director of the project, who is also a relative of the villager that wanted Abu Fu'ad's job, accompanied him. After complimenting Abu Fu'ad on his connections, the inspector told the local director that it seemed Abu Fu'ad's son was going to replace him in July. When the inspector had left, the local director said, "Milhim bayk (the man who employs Abu Fu'ad as a caretaker) is really working for you." Abu Fu'ad countered by saying that Milhim bayk didn't have a word in the matter; the credit (Ar. *faḍl*) went to the zaʿīm described above. "That way," as he told me afterward, "they know that they can't change a thing." Sure enough, when July came his son got the job.

This example illustrates several aspects of the ways relationships based on exchange have developed since the feudal period. First, it shows how factional boundaries can be crossed, and how ultimately they can be altered, through personal relationships based on exchange between the leader of one faction and people who traditionally would be followers in another. Abu Fu'ad had begun to dissociate himself from the alliances contracted by other members of his family long before the present example took place by aiding the leader of the faction opposed to his own during the fighting in 1958. That zaʿīm, seeking to weaken his political opponents by weaning away their supporters, reciprocated by providing wāsiṭa when Abu Fu'ad requested it. The present example illustrates a new phase in this recurring cycle of exchange between the two men. Here, the zaʿīm helps Abu Fu'ad even against one of his own traditional supporters. That is, the zaʿīm implies by his action that Abu Fu'ad is now on an equal footing with his traditional supporter and the same rules—that whoever asks for services first will get them—apply to both. Such an example shows all concerned that the boundaries between factions have, in effect, been redrawn and Abu Fu'ad is now openly counted among the clients of the zaʿīm.

Second, the example of Abu Fu'ad shows the margin of maneuver and choice which today is available even to a former peasant in the making of alliances. Abu Fu'ad has never learned to read or write and, as the example shows, even has to ask others to dial a telephone for him. Despite his lack of formal education, which precluded his getting a skilled job in the government or industry and lessened his chances to emigrate abroad, Abu Fu'ad learned a lot from his experience. That "education" served him well in showing how to exchange the rewards he possessed—political support, past military training, personal contacts, experience with the ways decisions were executed (but not made) according to formal administrative procedures —for the rewards he needed.

Third, the example of Abu Fu'ad shows clearly that a kind of wāsita is a key process in building and maintaining a political following. A potential follower may request that a zaʿīm use his influence to intercede on the requestor's behalf in some matter. If the zaʿīm delivers the service requested, the follower is "indebted" to him and should "repay" by manifesting support in visits to the zaʿīm's office or home, praising his character to others, voting for him in the next election, etc. As Abu Fu'ad and my other friend pointed out, the traditional factional affiliations in Barouk have been changed somewhat through one zaʿīm's ability to build a personal following by exchanging wasayiṭ for votes.

In national elections, when this zaʿīm is personally a candidate, he and his allies get the votes of most of his traditional supporters plus more than one-half of the votes cast by families belonging to the faction traditionally opposed to his own. In local elections, however, the traditional alliances are generally maintained, so the opposing faction has consistently dominated the town council.

Of course, this pattern of building support is characteristic not only of the village of Barouk. Rather, an extremely interesting article in the Lebanese weekly *Monday Morning* maintains that the process is ubiquitous:

> *Wasta* is everywhere. It permeates the private sector and the public sector, doing good in some instances and spreading havoc in others, building up "national leaders" and tying the hands of well-intentioned officials, pressuring the machinery of government to give people their rights and bending the law to give people what is not rightfully theirs. [Samaha 1974:7]

In this article, the reporter describes how she met with several important people in government and private life to find out what they thought about wāsiṭa. Several politicians expressed clearly the link between wāsiṭa and political support. One of them expressed it the following way:

> I love people and people love me—they are faithful to me. The fruits of my services were very evident last election season, when I got 33,000 votes. I enjoy helping people. People have got to live. To live, they have to have access to public servants, and without the help of politicians, they cannot gain access to them. [Samaha 1974:7]

It should be emphasized that most of the services referred to are personal, not public, services. That is, they concern helping someone to get a government permit for a new business, to have his child enrolled in a prestigious school, to arrange for a telephone, to find employment, to postpone legal action, etc., rather than bringing a hospital, a road, or an electricity project to the district which the politician represents. Thus, the exchange of service for support establishes a personal relationship between the requestor and the man who intercedes on his behalf. This relationship is often expressed in moral terms, as when one party speaks of the trust and loyalty, the faithfulness and sincerity, which he "owes" to the other.

A more serious treatment of the same phenomena gives a realistic and revealing example of the ways different kinds of exchange are perceived to lead to very different relationships:

> A young man, whose family has strongly supported Joseph Sakaf [a parliamentary deputy from the town of Zaḥli] for many years, but was also quite poor, especially in recent years, wanted to join the army. When he went to ask Sakaf to help him enroll in the army, he was refused on the grounds that he sold his vote to Sakaf in the last election. The young man protested vigorously that he had not done so and that although he was poor, he was honorable and had always voted for Sakaf out of loyalty. Sakaf then produced a list of people who according to one of his political agents had received payment for their votes. It included the man's name along with those of his brothers, sisters and mother. The youth promptly denounced it as a fabrication, whereupon Sakaf immediately telephoned the agent and requested him to come to his house. In the confrontation the political agent admitted that no one in the family had sold their votes and that he had pocketed the money. Sakaf apologized profusely to the young man and promptly helped him enter the army. [Gubser 1973:183]

The contrast between exchanging votes for money as opposed to exchanging votes for wāsiṭa is quite striking. Surely this is a clear example of the difference between economic exchange, which does not establish any further obligations or relationships but is terminated by the transaction, and social exchange, where the parties involved in the transaction establish a more enduring relationship based on the obligation to make future returns. In the example, Sakaf was called on to make a return for the support which the young man's family had extended him for years. Originally he felt that his obligations to them had already been fulfilled; when he learned this was not the case, he hastened to apologize and to make the return requested. Furthermore, the example shows how reciprocity is manifested in such a relationship: not as a tit-for-tat trade of vote for wāsiṭa, but as a series of prestations made over time by both parties so as to build up a "reserve fund" which can be drawn upon in times of need.

From the above it appears that the overall pattern which emerges from comparing leader-follower ties in feudal Mount Lebanon, on the one hand, and modern Lebanon, on the other hand, is a relative shift from alliances between families (e.g., the Yazbaki and Junblāṭṭi factions) to alliances between persons (e.g., a zaʿīm and his zilm). Whereas in the past most alliance relationships were based on exchanges between persons representing their families, at present they increasingly are based on exchanges between smaller parties—ultimately, between individuals. Expressed in terms of the categories proposed by Wolf (1966*a*:81-89), the shift is one from Type 4 coalitions ("descent groups") to Type 3 coalitions ("patron-client groups").

According to Wolf, a Type 4 coalition is many-stranded: its members are linked by several interests which manifest themselves in more than one domain of activity, e.g., in politics, marriage, visiting, etc. A Type 4 coalition also is vertical: it links members who are unequal in power because they do not control goods and/or services which are culturally equivalent in value. Finally, a Type 4 coalition is polyadic: it links many persons or many groups of persons.

A Type 3 coalition also is many-stranded and vertical. However, this kind of coalition differs from the preceding one in being dyadic: it links two persons or two groups of persons. Thus, the zaʿīm who built a personal following among the traditional supporters of his rivals in Barouk essentially broke the polyadic tie linking those supporters to his rivals and replaced it with a dyadic one linking them to him. The means by which he achieved this breakthrough was an exchange of his wasayiṭ for their votes and other manifestations of affiliation.

Of course, the change under discussion is a relative one. During the feudal period, most coalitions were of the Type 4 variety; at present, more Type 3 coalitions are found. This does not imply that factional divisions of the older style have completely disappeared; they certainly have not. For instance, residential sections and social interaction in many villages are still affected by them.

A manifestation of the effect of factions on social interaction showed up as field research was just beginning in Barouk. The small group of villagers with whom I had contact passed on the word from haddīk 'al-ḥāra: families belonging to the faction traditionally opposed to that of the man who lent me his house had decided not to help my research because they feared I might be a spy. I had expected there would be problems of this nature, given the factional division of the village, the recent war, and my outsider status. However, I was somewhat surprised at the effectiveness of the embargo. Aside from funerals, weddings, and one exchange of personal visits, I had no social contact with people from haddīk 'al-ḥāra.

As summer approached and, with it, the need for finding another house, I began to receive feelers about those available for rent. I was interested in finding something near the market, mainly because it was the nexus for residential boundaries between the factions, and therefore "neutral territory." Furthermore, I wanted to involve the small but growing number of villagers with whom I had established personal relations in the process of finding a new house. Hopefully, they would share in the change and thus be more likely to maintain relations even when we left their neighborhood. Several places in the same area were recommended to us, but we politely and repeatedly explained that they were fine places but far from the market, too big for us, etc. Finally one of the ladies suggested a couple of different places to my ex-wife. I asked Abu Karim, a friend, about them and he recommended one to us: three nice rooms, next to the market but with a balcony that gave onto the other side, toward the cedars. I asked who the owner was and, when I didn't recognize the name, Abu Karim added that I probably didn't know him because he was from haddīk 'al-ḥāra.

Later that week, Abu Karim, my ex-wife, and I had a look at the place and liked it. When we finished, my friend asked us to go ahead while he stayed to talk with the owner, a Druze šayk̲ 'ad-dīn, about prices. We bought a few things at the market and then headed home, where Abu Karim joined us. He said that the šayk̲ wanted a thousand Lebanese pounds (approximately $400.00) for the rest of the year. Since I had hoped to find a place for about six hundred pounds, I asked whether the rent might be lower if we promised to leave by the end of the summer (September 30). My friend said it might, so we went directly to speak with the owner. As we entered his shop, he greeted us and invited me to sit on the one free chair. I insisted that Abu Karim take it, but he refused and began explaining our conversation to the owner. He mentioned that he had told me what the šayk̲ had said and that I had asked whether he might be willing to rent only to the end of September, instead of to the end of the year. The šayk̲ said of course he would be willing to do that.

"How much would you like for that period?" I asked.

"Eight hundred pounds."

"Could you give it to us for six hundred?"

"No, it's not possible. (Silence.) People have already come to rent the place for a whole year, but I don't want to let anyone take it that long. I only want good people (Ar. 'awādim) like you, but I can get more than six hundred pounds from someone who comes for only two months in the summer."

A Syrian who was working in the village as a laborer came into the shop. He effusively greeted all present and we returned the greetings; it was obvious that he had been drinking and was in a jovial mood.

Abu Karim said, "May I say a word for you, Mr. Fred; can I come into the matter, šayk̲?"

I said, "Go ahead"; the šayk̲ just looked at him.

Abu Karim returned the look and continued, "You know I'm getting nothing out of this, but Mr. Fred is a good man and you are a good man, so I want to make a wāsiṭa. Why don't we take half from you and half from him and finish for seven hundred pounds?"

The Syrian said, "Yes, everybody in the village knows Abu Karim is a good man, no one like him in the village, a very good man."

Abu Karim asked, "What do you say, our šayḵ?"

The šayḵ shook his head and turned his face away but seemed hesitant.

Abu Karim took my hand and said, "Here is the hand of Mr. Fred; where is your hand, o šayḵ?"

The šayḵ put his hand behind his back.

The Syrian laughed, came over, and said, "Come on, šayḵ, half and half" (Ar. *nuṣṣ bin-nuṣṣ*) and he grabbed the šayḵ's hand and pulled it into mine.

The šayḵ said, "Only for your sake (Ar. *kurmāllak*), Abu Karim; I don't want to do it, but only for your sake."

I stood up and shook hands with the owner. He leaned forward and kissed me on the cheek, saying, "May the arrangement be blessed" (Ar. *mabrūk*). I kissed him in return and said, "May God bless you" (Ar. *'allah yabārik fīk*).

We then agreed on how the money was to be paid and Abu Karim and I left the shop. I invited him for a drink to celebrate the deal, and when we got home we told my ex-wife, May, how it had been concluded. She was less than excited about it but didn't have time to explain because just then another couple arrived to pay us a visit. After we had exchanged greetings and social pleasantries, we told them why we were celebrating and invited them to join us. As their glasses were filled, they of course wanted all the details. Abu Karim described the house and then asked the man how much he thought it was worth for the summer. He said he didn't know—maybe five or six hundred—how much did we pay? Abu Karim said we paid more; the visitor guessed eight hundred. Abu Karim countered with "less," and the visitor concluded that it must be seven hundred, which was a good price both for the owner and for us. May said she thought the price was high because her parents had rented a much better house in another village for only a little more.

"When did they rent for that price?" asked Abu Karim.

"In the past, I don't know exactly when."

"Everything is getting more expensive these days," said Abu Karim.

May answered, "Yes, but I'm afraid that the šayḵ asked for more when he saw Fred was an American and he thought, as we Lebanese do, that all Americans are rich and foolish."

Abu Karim denied this, saying, "I spoke to him about that and told him that you were good people but not rich, that Mr. Fred was still a student doing research here on how the people of the village live together."

May said that she still wished I had waited until talking with her father. Abu Karim countered by saying, "You still have paid no money, so I can go to tell the šayḵ that the deal is off and you can look around for another place. I'd prefer that, myself."

I answered, "No, I like the house. I feel we paid a good price for it, a price we couldn't have gotten without your help. Besides I gave my word, so I won't change it now." Talk then turned to other matters, and after a while, Abu Karim left.

When I saw him the next day, he was still irritated and wanted to cancel the deal. He stressed that he was getting nothing from it, that it might even cost him something: "The šayḵ said he accepted the price only for my sake, so he can ask me to do something for him in the future." I tried to soothe him, saying that I liked the house very much and appreciated his help in getting it, as I had told the visitors when he was there. "All right," said Abu Karim, "only you and Yusif bayk (the man in whose house we were staying at the time) are important to me. We won't talk about it any more."

This series of events provides a clear example of how relationships based on mutual social exchange can sometimes be used to bridge boundaries between different groups. Abu Karim was a friend of mine; he was a fellow villager of the šayḵ who had the house for rent. Thus, Abu Karim was linked by ties of friendship, on the one hand, and neighborliness, on the other. On the basis of these relationships he interceded on my behalf to explain our financial situation and to assure the šayḵ that we were "good people" to have in his house. During the actual bargaining session, he asked permission from both parties to enter the negotiations and then proposed a fifty-fifty compromise. Actually, it was clear to all concerned that Abu Karim was more partial to me; the šayḵ put it on the record by emphasizing that he was accepting the compromise only for Abu Karim's sake. Having thus extended himself for our friendship, Abu Karim was irritated by what he perceived to be a lack of gratitude on our part, especially when it occurred in front of other villagers. Thus, he served notice that he wished to absolve his responsibility in the matter by cancelling the deal. That way, even if he had insufficient gratitude from us for his help, still he would not be "indebted" to the šayḵ for a favor. His irritation was mollified somewhat by my manifestations of gratitude, both publicly and privately expressed, but it did not disappear until he indicated that a good word to his patron would be appreciated. One good turn deserved another, so to speak.

With Abu Karim's help, then, we were able to find a new house, and we began to develop relations with the owner and his family. Through them, and others, we also learned of a young man who was studying in the United States and having a hard time of it. Members of the young man's extended family contacted me by telephone and visits, and I wrote some letters to couples we knew in the city where he was studying. I gave them his address and phone number and asked them to look after him, introduce him around, etc. Unfortunately, we learned about the situation too late to be of much help, since the young man got sick, abandoned his studies, and returned to Lebanon. However, it seems his family appreciated our attempt to help, and that appreciation facilitated our contacts with others living in their residential section.

Another approach to broadening relations throughout the village was by contacting people close to the leader of the faction with whom I had few contacts as yet. My then father-in-law and I visited the personal secretary of a political leader and he got in touch with a friend and associate of the zaʿīm concerned. This man had been associated with the zaʿīm for a long time and he also was a "son-in-law of the village" (Ar. *ṣuhr 'aḍ-ḍay'a*) of Barouk, since he had married a woman belonging to one of the families there. After visiting us in Beirut, and then inviting us to their summer home in the mountains, this man and his wife were extremely helpful in many ways. First, they contacted people they knew in the village, explained what we were doing and why (stressing that I was a student doing ordinary research for a degree, with no secret connections to the U.S. government or any company), and asked those people to help us. Second, they went over a questionnaire that I planned to administer in the village and recommended certain changes to make it more relevant, accurate, and acceptable to the people who would answer it. Third, they visited us in the village and publicly manifested their support for us and the study we were doing.

As our contacts broadened throughout Barouk, then, I began to get help with my research. Several members of the local cultural and social club (Ar. *nādi 'aṭ-ṭaqāfi 'al-'ijtimāʿi lis̆-s̆abāb 'al-barūk*) agreed to help in interviewing. This club had been functioning in the village for more than ten years, I was told, and currently had a membership of about fifty young people (up to around age 35). While a real attempt was made to recruit members from all families, sects, and political groups in the village, those from families belonging to one faction did constitute a majority and had preponderant influence in the club. The overall goal which members worked toward was the good of the community of Barouk. For instance, they organized a scouting group and a football team for the village during the summer of 1974. In previous years, they had invited speakers from various parties to discuss the Lebanese political situation at forums open to the public. Also, one summer they organized a festival at the cedars where nationally-known entertainers appeared. Tickets were sold for this affair and the proceeds went to help the club's activities and to rent the building where they hold meetings every weekend during the summer and once a month during the winter. Currently the club is financed mainly from the sale of calendars and from a benefit which the members put on in the village market street once a year.[13]

In early September, those members of the club who had agreed to help us met to discuss the questionnaire. I had already given five interviews in a test run, gotten reactions, and incorporated some of them as changes in the form of the questionnaire. I began the discussion by reminding everyone of what I had come to study in Barouk and how this questionnaire was a part of that overall effort. Then I asked the others to read through their copies of the questionnaire as May and I play-acted an interview, her asking and me answering. When the others had a question or comment, or when we wanted to stress a point or technique (e.g., how to probe), we stopped the demonstration and discussed the matter.

The volunteers from the club strongly recommended one major change in the questionnaire. It concerned a question which asked whether the respondent felt that the people of the village could be subdivided into four classes: the notables (Ar. *'al-wujahā'*), those who are well off (Ar. *'al-mubaḥbaḥīn*), those who can keep up appearances (Ar. *'al-mastūrīn*), and the poor (Ar. *'al-fuqarā'*).[14] What, they asked, about the example of someone

[13]The benefit held during the summer of 1974 included a skit which indicated important differences between the ways members of the youth club, as contrasted with their elders, conceive of and evaluate the dealings between a za'īm and his zilm. In this skit, a peasant so poor that he could offer only water as hospitality was visited by a friend. He and the friend began talking about the peasant's fine son, a new schoolteacher, when an inspector arrived to say the peasant's water would be cut off unless he paid his bill. The peasant insisted that the water belonged to his village, where God made it come out of the mountain; besides, he had no money to pay. When the inspector and the friend left, the peasant decided that the only course of action was to visit his za'īm and ask for help. Act two of the skit took place in the office of the za'īm, who sat behind a table holding a riding crop and wearing a fancy jacket, an open-collared shirt, and sunglasses. The za'īm talked briefly about how well things were going for him, through his contacts in the government and control of the poor. He was visited by his chief henchman (Ar. *qabaḍay*), who asked where to put all the surplus riches they were getting. Then the poor peasant was admitted and he addressed the za'īm as "our lord, Sa'īd bey" (Ar. *sīdnā Sa'īd bayk*). The peasant explained his problem and asked for help; the za'īm said the only thing he could do was buy the peasant's land. The peasant didn't want to sell but the za'īm insisted. Then the peasant's son burst in and told his father they had no business being in such a "low place" (Ar. *maḥall waṭī*). The za'im was enraged by this insult and called in his henchman to throw them out. In the ensuing struggle, the son dealt with the henchman, while the peasant flattened the za'īm with his walking stick. The son then shouted out to the audience "O you the people, do as my father did!" (Ar. *yā 'intum 'aš-ša'b 'amilū mitil mā 'amil bayyī*), as the curtain fell to rousing applause. Whether this skit only dramatizes a sophomoric misunderstanding of political realities, or actually foreshadows the wave of the future as youth club members take on responsibility and power in the village, remains to be seen.

[14]These categories were taken directly from another study of social stratification in a Lebanese village (Khuri 1969).

who comes from the mušāyik̲ but now has no money, education, or influence: is he one of the notables or one of the poor? Or conversely, what about someone who now has a high position but whose parents were very poor and without social distinction? To deal with these recommendations, we divided the question into four parts: one asking for the respondent's opinion about how many social classes there were in Barouk; a second asking the same about economic classes; and the last two asking for the names of the respective social and economic classes.

That decided, each of the four volunteers from the club took twenty questionnaires and agreed to give them to members of his or her own family. Later on, two other young men joined in the effort, so there were eight people, including May and myself, involved in giving the questionnaire during the first month. As the others completed their copies, they returned them to us. I read through them quickly, checking that all questions had been answered and getting a rough overview of how the whole project was going. I accompanied one young man as he did a few interviews in order to give him pointers on how to conduct them. May, who has worked as a professional interviewer in Lebanon, did the same with two young ladies. Later, as the new school year began, our helpers became too involved in other things to continue administering interviews, but their help in the beginning was very valuable. Not only did they enable us to contact quickly a much larger number of households, but also they gave the whole project a local identification, since members of the village were helping to carry it through.

Generally the interviewer appeared at a residence, without having made a prior appointment, and asked to speak with the head of the household. If the head was present,[15] the interviewer gave a brief explanation about my work and the questionnaire–brief, because word got around very fast what we were doing–and then asked the head if he was willing to participate. If he was, and most were, the interviewer asked all the questions in the order they were arranged in the questionnaire. All questions were asked in colloquial Arabic, and answers were written down in Arabic immediately, in front of the respondent, so that he knew how his answers were recorded.[16] Filling out a questionnaire took anywhere from twenty minutes to two hours, depending on the respondent, with most averaging around a half hour. The last page of the questionnaire, which deals with the time, date, and general environment of the interview, could be written on the spot or just after leaving the household.

---

[15] If the head of the household was not present, generally an appointment was made to meet with him in the near future. When that meeting took place, the same procedures as outlined above were followed.

[16] A translation of the questionnaire is given as Appendix 1.

Originally I had offered to pay interviewers or make a contribution to the club in their names. Both of these offers were refused, so neither respondents nor interviewers received any remuneration from the project. Interviewing began in September, was continued through October by May and myself, and by me through December. In all, 149 questionnaires were completed, with a deliberate attempt being made to gather data from all the families of the village.

According to the records of the national election in 1972, the 341 families registered to vote in Barouk were divided into six groups–three for men and three for women. Groups 1 (men) and 4 (women) were composed of people from 70 Christian families belonging to both factions; Groups 2 (men) and 5 (women), of people from 100 Druze and 70 Christian families of the Yazbaki faction; and Groups 3 (men) and 6 (women), of people from 101 Druze families of the Junblāṭṭi faction. To make the questionnaire sample representative of these divisions in the real population, therefore, three questionnaires for Junblāṭṭi Druze households (i.e., those belonging to the groups which had been interviewed more than their "share") were deselected in a random manner from further processing. This provided a set of data which represented sectarian and factional divisions in the real population able to vote within 99% confidence limits.

As a casual reading of Appendix 1 shows, the questionnaire elicited the standard sort of census information about sexes, ages, residences, educations, and jobs of all members in each household. The income, expenses, personal and productive property owned by members of the household also were examined. Attitudinal information about social and economic classes in the village was then requested, as well as information on association membership, marriage choices, and visiting patterns.

The information on visiting patterns was of major importance in delineating social stratification. As was explained earlier, almost all social life in the village is effected through making and receiving visits, which are organized into three major types: visits for social obligations (Ar. *ziyāra lal-wājib*), visits without ceremony (Ar. *ziyāra bidūn taklīf*), and visits for a particular interest (Ar. *ziyāra lal-maṣlaḥa*).

The ways in which visits of the three categories are exchanged indicate the relationships which hold between the parties concerned. As was discussed earlier, visits for social obligations are closely regulated according to the principle of reciprocity: if A goes to a funeral in B's family, B is expected to make a return visit when a funeral occurs in A's family. Visits without ceremony, in contrast, are not "counted" (Ar. *maḥsūb*) in the same way: A may visit B many times before receiving a return. Of course, in actual social life, just where one draws the line limiting accpetable behavior is subject to individual variation: one can always be "understanding" about others, especially when they are "close to the heart" (Ar. *qarīb 'al-qalb*), but there usually comes a point where enough is enough and an accounting is demanded. Visits for a particular interest also seem less subject to the principle of reciprocity but in fact only the form of the return changes: A's visit to B is "compensated for" by B's attempt to deliver the interest–i.e., the goods or services–sought by A. The apparent similarity between visits without cost and those for a particular interest–neither seemingly subject to the principle of reciprocity–actually provides the parties concerned with a face-saving way of talking about the exchanges they are making. It is socially more appropriate for fellow villagers to be seen as close friends rather than parties to an exchange relationship, let alone as superiors and subordinates.

As one strips away the surface similarity, however, the realities of social stratification become evident. When one says he usually is visited but does not visit, he makes a claim to superiority over those who visit him. Conversely, when one says he visits without being visited in return, he affirms his subordination to those he visits. Finally, those who say they sometimes visit without receiving visits in return are claiming a middle status, neither wholly superior nor subordinate but sometimes one and sometines the other.

The sensitivity of information thus revealed so starkly by exchanges of visits, I feel, was a major reason behind the opposition we encountered in getting responses to the section on visiting in the questionnaire. More household heads refused to answer this part of the questionnaire than any other. Furthermore, some people objected quite vocally to our even asking for this sort of information.

Once a young man we knew came to visit us with a friend of his. Our friend kept very quiet and seemed nervous, while the other young man talked very loudly and rapidly and seemed extremely forward for a first visit. He explained that he was one of our neighbors and then quickly launched into a series of pointed questions about the project we had several of his friends doing around the village. For instance, he had heard that we said people were visiting others and not being visited back, and what did we think we meant by that? We straightened this gentleman out by reading the question verbatim, thus showing that we had asked whether such a visiting pattern occurred, not asserted that it did. This seemed to take some of the steam out of him, and both he and our friend then offered to help us. I tried to make an appointment when we could meet to discuss the questionnaire and how it should be given, but our neighbor was so busy that it was impossible to set a convenient time. The young man we knew before, on the other hand, did set and keep an appointment for this purpose, but he was drafted into the army before he could take an active role in making interviews.

On another occasion, I was starting to ask a respondent the questions about visiting when his son entered the room. He listened intently as I asked whether the head of the household usually visited other people in the village who did not return his visits. The father said "yes;" the son said, "No, you don't" and wanted to know what was going on, what all these questions were about. I repeated the introduction which I had given earlier to his father, and he told his son that there was nothing to worry about, that we were visiting everyone in the village to ask these questions. Accordingly, I again asked the father the same question and he said, yes, he did, a little. The son then corrected his father a second time, saying that no, he did not, because today everyone must return visits in order to be visited. It was not like the old days, when the feudal lords were visited by everyone but they didn't visit anybody except other lords. Then he asked whether I had encountered anyone who said that sometimes visits were not returned; I said that I had. Which way, he wanted to know; both ways, I said, since some people claimed they were visited but didn't visit and others said they visited but were not visited in return. "It's not true," he said: "the visit is returned" (Ar. *'az-ziyāra mutabādali*). "Of course, you have to keep in mind the duties of the persons involved: somebody may visit me two or three times before I can visit him back because I'm busy." I said I understood that but was asking about the usual patterns, not exceptions. "The custom is that visits are returned," he said. Thereafter, his father answered no to all further questions about differences in exchanging visits.

As a further example, once I was discussing some completed interviews with the two young men who had given them. I noticed that there seemed to be some inconsistent information in answers to the visiting questions. For instance, several persons had indicated in response to one question that they visited for particular interests; however, later they claimed that they did not make visits which were unanswered by return visits. I said I had thought that a visit for a particular interest usually was not answered by a return visit. "That's right," they both agreed. Then one of them added, "Most people make visits for particular interests but no one likes to talk about them."

As a final example, one of the young ladies helping us once brought several completed interviews to the house. She had coffee with us as I looked through them and asked about points which weren't clear in some of the answers. She provided the information requested; then she added, "You have to remember that these answers are only approximate, not exact." I said probably that was especially true of the answers about income, expenses, and land ownership. "No, I think those answers are pretty accurate," she said. I asked what points she was referring to then. She answered, "I mean the ones on classes, marriages, and visiting; people don't usually like to talk about such things in the village." (This same young woman had, on an earlier visit, wondered how the mušāyik̲ were answering these questions, whether they were trying to be different from the other villagers, etc.)

Responses to the questions on visiting, then, gave a clear key to stratification patterns in the village. If a head said his household was visited by people from inside or outside Barouk but it did not return those visits—i.e., if he answered "yes" to questions 46 and/or 50—the household was a candidate for visiting set 3. If, in addition, the reasons given for those visits and the relationship existing between his household and the visitors were not "exceptional," then his household was placed in that set—i.e., those who received visits which they usually did not return. An "exceptional" reason might be, for instance, because someone in the home was sick and therefore he or she received visits but was unable to return them. In a lighter vein, an "exceptional" relationship listed by one informant was the one holding between his household and the electricity meter man, who visited him regularly without ever receiving a return visit. Thirty-three households fulfilled these criteria and thus were placed in visiting set 3—i.e., those who regularly received visits which they did not return.

Other households, in contrast, said that they made visits which were not returned by people inside or outside the village—i.e., they answered "yes" to questions 47 and/or 51. If there was nothing "exceptional" about the reasons for these visits and the relationships holding between the parties visiting and being visited, then the household was placed in visiting set 1. Examples of "exceptional" reasons were ones like "visiting a sick relative that we love very much," or "I have a car but my friend doesn't." An "exceptional" relationship reported by the man responsible for the humorous example above was "I sometimes visit the doctor but he never comes to see me." Eighteen households were placed in this set—i.e., those who make visits which are not usually returned.

Finally, still other households said that they both received visits which they usually didn't return and made visits which were usually not returned. That is, they answered "yes" to questions 46 and 47 and/or questions 50 and 51. Again, if there was nothing "exceptional" about the reasons for these visits or the relationships concerned, the household was placed in visiting set 2—i.e., those who both receive and make visits which are usually unreciprocated by return visits. Eleven households went into this set.

These three visiting sets provide a key to stratifications patterns in the village, but in themselves are an insufficient measure of socio-economic class membership. After all, only 62 of the 146 households interviewed actually placed themselves in this grid. Probably because of the sensitivity of the information concerned, 84 households either refused to answer the questions about visiting or claimed they had nothing to do with unreciprocated visits. It may be true that some of those 84 really do not receive or make such visits; however, I know that many of the households concerned did in fact visit others without receiving return visits from them because I was present on occasions when such visits were made. Still, the problem remains of how to translate the stratification patterns implied by exchanges of visits into indices which are applicable to the whole village. Furthermore, it is necessary to examine how such patterns correlate with more common indices used to determine socio-economic class membership —e.g., income, land ownership, education, etc.[17] Relying solely on these more common criteria, conversely, leads to the problem of how to establish non-arbitrary boundaries between the classes concerned, especially when continuous variables like income are examined.

One way of dealing with these considerations is to combine the two types of indices: one can determine what are the mean amounts of income, land owned, and education for each of the three visiting sets. Then one can determine the midpoints between these means and use those midpoints as class boundaries on each of the indices concerned. For example, the yearly mean income for visiting set 3 is 24,670 L.L. (Lebanese pounds); for visiting set 2, it is 15,260 L.L.; and for visiting set 1, it is 9070 L.L. The midpoint between sets 3 and 2 is 19,970 L.L.; that between sets 2 and 1 is 12,200 L.L. Thus any household which has a yearly income of less than 12,200 L.L. is in income set 1; any household with one of 19,970 L.L. or more per year is in income set 3; and any household with a yearly income between these two figures is in income set 2. In addition to income, owned land which produces a cash crop or other revenue (e.g., rent) and the education of the head of the household can be studied in this way. For example, any household with less than 1300 square meters of such land, either around Barouk or elsewhere in Lebanon, is in land-owner set 1; anyone with 3500 square meters or more is in land-owner set 3, and so forth. With regard to the level of education of the head of the household, there was no significant difference between the means for visiting sets 1 and 2, so anyone with more than a primary school education was in the upper of two education sets. To these indices of class membership may be added those of the occupation(s) of the head of the household (or, if he is retired, his former occupation) and the residential pattern of the household (i.e., whether it resides in the village only during summers, during weekends and holidays throughout the year as well as during summers, or during the whole year.) A particular household, then, was determined to belong to socio-economic class I, II, or III (lower to upper) depending on its characteristics in reference to all

[17]See Armstrong and Hirabayashi (1956), Berger (1964), Hakim (1966), Khuri (1969), and Prothro (1961) for other treatments of socio-economic class in Lebanon and in the Middle East generally.

these criteria–visiting, income, land ownership, residence in the village, and both the education and the occupation(s) of its head. When indices were conflicting (e.g., a household in visiting set 2, but income set 3, land-owner set 3, education set 1, etc.), the income and, if available, the visiting indices were given greater weight. Figure 3 presents all of this information in a tabular listing of socio-economic class placements.

Figure 3
Socio-Economic Classes in Barouk

Classes	Number of Households	% of Total Sample
I ("lower")	95	65
II ("middle")	39	27
III ("upper")	12	8
Totals	146	100%

I originally had planned to check this ranking of the socio-economic classes of households in two ways. First, I would compare my judgments with respondents' answers to questions 36 (the number and names of social and economic classes in the village), 37 (the respondents' self-placements in social and economic classes), and 38 (the influential people in the village). Second, I would classify households in terms of respondents' answers to questions 41 (whether there were families in the village into which the respondent's son, but not his daughter, could marry) and 42 (vice-versa) into four marriage sets: those whose sons, but not daughters, could so marry ("upper class"); those whose daughters, but not sons, could so marry ("lower class"); those who answered "yes" to both questions ("middle class"); and those who answered "no" to both ("indeterminate"). These data could be subjected to the same operations as the visiting sets were before: that is, they could be correlated with income, land ownership, etc.; then the "marriage sets" could be contrasted with the visiting sets to see if essentially the same picture of social stratification emerged.

Unfortunately, I worded questions 41 and 42 incorrectly for this task. The cultural "reason" underlying this ranking of marriage sets is that in Barouk, as well as in the Middle East generally, the wife usually takes on the social attributes of her husband.[18] Thus, a man can marry "down,"

[18] Two interesting and well-informed studies of marriages in Lebanon are Alameddin (1975), for Druze customs, and Fredericks (1974), for Christian ones. Also M. Ayoub (1957) is still highly valuable.

maintain his own status, and elevate that of his wife; however, when a man marries "up," he keeps the same status and lowers that of his wife. Interestingly, the same rule applies in an analogous fashion to religion: in a marriage between two people who formerly were members of different sects, the woman generally takes on the religion of the man. It is necessary for at least one of them to change, because there is no civil marriage in Lebanon. Thus, I worded questions 41 and 42 ambiguously for my purposes. A respondent may have answered these questions according to class criteria, or according to sectarian criteria, or one time one and the other time the other. It now seems extremely difficult to pin down which variable determined a given respondent's answers, or even if in fact only one was on his mind at the time. If I had prefaced questions 41 and 42 with the phrase "within your own sect," the problem would have been avoided. Since the questions were flawed, however, I was not able to carry out this check of the socio-economic class placements.

Figure 4
Cross Tabulation of Self-Placements (SP)
and Researcher's Placement (RP) of Households

RP	I		II		III	
SP	S′	E′	S′	E′	S′	E′
Category 1	29	10	25	0	0	0
Category 2	29	73	49	85	58	67
Category 3	3	3	13	10	25	33
Other	16	6	5	0	17	0
No Answer	22	8	8	5	0	0
Totals	100	100	100	100	100	100
N	95	95	39	39	12	12

Note: Since respondents answered in terms of social classes (S) and economic classes (E), it is necessary to present information about both as subcategories of the socio-economic classes I, II, and III.

The comparison of respondents' self-placements with my placement of their households in the three-class system was more productive, as is shown in Figure 4. If the two groups of placements are similar, one would expect most households to lie along a diagonal from the upper left corner (category 1, class I) to the middle right side (category 3, class III) of Figure 4. This expectation is only roughly supported by the actual data: there is a gradual shift of self-placements from (lower) class I, to (middle) class II, to (upper) class III as one reads across the figure from left to right. A major consideration underlying Figure 4, of course, is how respondents' answers were grouped into the self-placement categories, since they could use any terms they wished to designate any number of classes they felt were present. Figure 5 presents a list of the Arabic terms used by respondents (plus English glosses for them) and shows how they were grouped into each category.

Perhaps one factor causing the correlation of class placements to be less pronounced than expected is the refusal of many respondents to categorize their households. If so, the patterning of these refusals is instructive: 22% of those I placed in the lower class declined to answer, but only 8% of the middle class and none of the upper class did so. A second factor tending to blur the correlation of class placements could be the tendency of many villagers to opt for the comfortable ambiguity of the expression "middle class" (Ar. *'aṭ-ṭabaqa 'al-mutawassiṭa*). As some explained after so designating their households, "we are no better than anyone nor worse than anyone" (Ar. *lā niḥnā 'aḥsan min haddan wa lā niḥnā 'a'ṭal min haddan*).

Stronger support for the proposed placements of households in the three-class system is provided by Figure 6. In answering question 38, a respondent could name as many "influential persons in Barouk" as he saw fit. Some named none; at least one named sixteen. Nineteen men from the 146 households analyzed were named as "influentials." Of these, three belonged to households in class I; six in class II; and eight in class III. An even more accurate measure of influence, though, was the number of respondents who chose to name any one individual. The "votes" in this regard are heavily in favor of persons in class III: all five men who were named most often by respondents are in this class; as well, the total number of times each man was named is significant. Thus, the man judged to be the most influential in the village had almost twice as many "votes" as his closest rival. Furthermore, the number of votes received by all influentials in class III far surpasses that of the other two classes, totalling more than 86% of all "votes" cast. Finally, eight of the twelve households (67%) in class III possess a man considered to be influential, compared with six of the thirty-nine (15%) in class II, and three of the ninety-five (3%) in class I. Clearly, differences of this degree indicate that the respondents' ratings of influential people in the village support the household placements proposed.

It must be emphasized that these socio-economic class rankings pertain to the village of Barouk, and no claim is made that they are representative of the Lebanese population at large. Before similar intensive research is done in other Lebanese environments, especially in the cities, such a claim would be foolhardy. Earlier in this section, comment was made about the questionable statistical evidence available on Lebanon, but such evidence

Figure 5
Groupings of Arabic Terms Used by Respondents
into Self-Placement Categories

Categories	Arabic Term	English Gloss
Social		
(a) Category 1:	ʿādīya	"ordinary"
	ʿāmmīya	"common"
	mitʿallimīn basīṭ	"slightly educated"
	muṯaqafīn basīṭ	"slightly educated"
(b) Category 2:	mutawassiṭa	"middle"
	wusṭā	"middle"
	mitʿallimīn	"educated"
	muṯaqafīn	"cultured"
(c) Category 3:	mušāyiḵ	"sheiks"
	bakawāt	"beys"
	ʿalīya	"high"
	wujahā'	"notables"
	rafīʿa	"refined"
	maʿrūfi	"well known"
(d) Other:	All other terms used by informants to denote social classes	
Economic		
(a) Category 1:	faqīra	"poor"
	waṭī	"low"
	ʿawaz	"needy"
	muḥtāji	"needy"
	karihīn	"in a disagreeable state"
(b) Category 2:	mastūra	"able to keep up appearances"
	maysūra	"lower middle"
	mutawassiṭa	"middle"
	wusṭā	"middle"
	murtaḥīn	"comfortable"
	mubaḥbaḥīn	"well off"
(c) Category 3:	malīya	"wealthy"
	ġanīya	"rich"
	rās māli	"capitalistic"
	ʿalīya	"high"
	wujahā'	"notables"
	rafīʿa	"refined"
	'iqtāʿīya	"feudal lords"
	maʿrūfi	"well known"
(d) Other	All other terms used by respondents to denote economic classes	

Figure 6
Cross-Tabulation of Respondents' Choices about Influential People in Barouk (IPB) with Researcher's Placements (RP) of Village Households[1]

RP	I	II	III
IPB			
1.			56
2.			31
3.			26
4.			23
5.			19
6.	9		
7.			6
8.	5		
9.		4	
10.		2	
11.		2	
12.-18.	1	1	1
		1	1
		1	
N:	15	11	163

[1]N=times mentioned, from most to least frequently.

as exists would indicate that stratification in Barouk is not representative of that in the nation as a whole. For instance, Issawi (1966) bases much of his discussion of the inequality of income distribution in Lebanon on a table, which has been reproduced as Figure 7.

Figure 7[1]
Table of Income Distribution in Lebanon in 1959-60

Income Classes	% of Families	Below LL per annum	Average Annual Income LL	% Gross National Product
Wretched	8.8	1200	1000	1.8
Poor	41.2	2500	2000	16.5
Medium	32.0	5000	3500	22.4
Well Off	14.0	15,000	10,000	28.0
Rich	4.0	above 15,000	40,000	32.0

[1]Issawi (1966:77). Both the title of the table and the text of Issawi's discussion make it clear that he is talking about income distribution, not per capita GNP.

If the information presented pertains to a discussion of income distribution, it is difficult to understand why the last column of figures expresses "% of Gross National Product." The relevant percentages to such a discussion concern disposable income, not production figures. Inferring, therefore, that the subtitle presented in Issawi's table is a misprint, a comparison becomes possible between income distribution in Lebanon during 1959-60 and that in Barouk during 1974. Figure 8 Presents a Lorenz curve of this information and it clearly shows an important variation in the upper ranges of the curve. The significance of these variations is that income is more equitably distributed in Barouk than it was in Lebanon generally. For instance, the top 10% of the population controlled 47.5% of Lebanese disposable income in 1959-60 but "only" 34% of it in Barouk in 1974.[19] Furthermore, the mean household income for the Barouk sample was 14,000 L.L. (about $6300) per year, while that for the national sample in 1959-60 was 5032 L.L. (about $2250).[20] Thus, it is unlikely that the class boundaries relevant in Barouk would be isometric with those in Lebanese society generally, but a final resolution of this point awaits further research.

SUMMARY

The discussion of class boundaries closes this section of the monograph, in which relevant aspects of the ethnographic context of field research have been described. An important focus of this description was visiting—the major vehicle by which social life is carried on in Barouk. Visits were categorized into those made for social obligations (especially mourning ceremonies and marriages), those made without ceremony or cost, and those made for a particular interest or benefit. Whereas visits in the first two categories generally establish and express relationships based on mutual social exchange, those in the last one may establish and express relationships based on power social exchange. The roots of such relationships go very deep into Lebanese history, as was shown by the comparison of social ties in feudal Lebanon with those existing today. A major difference between the two is that during feudal times these ties were based on exchanges of physical protection for support, while today they more often involve exchanges of personal services for support, with the institutions of national

[19] According to the Organization for Economic Cooperation and Development (1976) comparative figures for 1974 are 26.1% for the United States, 30.6% for Germany (Federal Republic).

[20] More recent figures concerning income distribution indicate that in 1973 the estimated per capita income for all Lebanese was $730.00 (U.S. Department of State 1975:1). Multiplying this figure by an average household size of seven persons produces a total of $5110 per year, which can be more relevantly compared to the mean household income in Barouk.

Figure 8
Lorenz Curve of Disposable Income in Lebanon[1] Generally in 1959-60 and in Barouk[2] in 1974

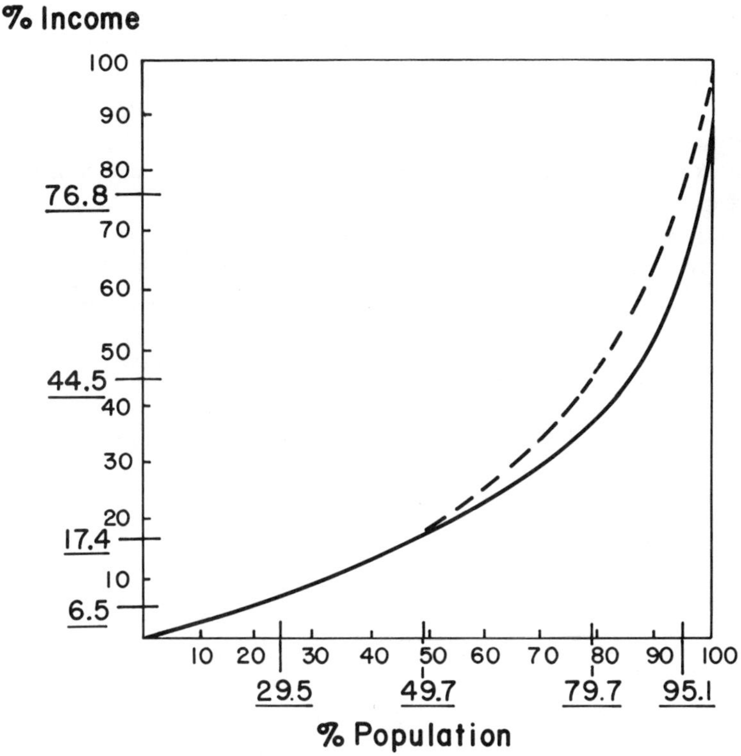

[1] See Figure 7 regarding the relevant percentages of disposable income and population for Lebanon generally.
[2] Underlined numbers denote the relevant percentages of disposable income and population for Barouk.

government—especially the army and police—taking a greater role in, and responsibility for, physical protection. A second major difference is that during the feudal period exchanges tended to be between families, while today they tend to be between smaller social units, even between individuals.

In short, the discussion has given examples of what wāsiṭa is and how it is used as a reward traded in social exchange in order to establish and/or change either mutual relationships or power relationships. Discussion thus far has also indicated how different parties conceive of the ways it is so used by describing their actions and presenting their commentaries on what they were doing and why. As was shown in Section 1, informant conceptions are exceedingly important to the social exchange model: they operate in a "secondary exchange" to permit judgments of the fairness or rightness of a given transaction and, by extension, of the parties involved in that transaction. The discussion in Section 1 also showed that informant conceptions of designative, as well as evaluative, meaning are important to the social exchange model, since they indicate which goods, services, and/or other "assets" are seen as "similar" or "synonymous with" culturally valued rewards. Because informant conceptions are so important in the prediction and explanation of behavior according to the social exchange model, more attention and study needs to be paid to them. In reference to the concerns of this particular monograph, more attention must be paid to how informants conceive of wāsiṭa. This will be done in the following section.

III

PSYCHOLINGUISTIC EXPERIMENT

Consistent with the theoretical requirements stated in Section 1 and with the ethnographic description in Section 2, we seek now to show how local informants in Barouk conceive of what the wāsiṭa process is and how it may be used. This will be accomplished by the discussion of a psycholinguistic experiment performed by a quota sample of Barouk's inhabitants, that is, a sample reflecting the various divisions of local society in their relative proportions. The discussion will proceed by the following stages: (1) choice of the sample of local informants; (2) choice of the terms for study; (3) administration of the experiment; (4) analyses of experimental results; and (5) summary and conclusions.

CHOICE OF INFORMANT SAMPLE

The original plan included completing the collection and analysis of household interviews before beginning the psycholinguistic experiment. Interview responses would then provide a basis for choosing a random sample of informants and the experiment would be administered to that sample.

However, field conditions required revision of the original plan. For the reasons discussed above, interviewing did not begin until September. Since the members of the youth club who helped with this task refused to accept payment for their services, only verbal encouragement could be used to speed their efforts. Increasingly, the burden for doing the interviews fell on May and me; by late October I was working alone. Increasingly, also, the villagers began to show that they were unwilling or unable to cooperate further. More people began making excuses why they couldn't do the interview at the time requested and refusing either to make, or to keep, appointments for doing it later. A straightforward refusal to cooperate was extremely rare; in my case, it happened only once. Such a refusal would have caused personal shame to all parties concerned: to the interviewer, through a public rejection of his request; to the interviewee, through his overt breach of hospitality; and to the "family of the village," through the clear display of differences of feeling and action within the local population. Rather, the appearance of smooth relations was maintained by a gradual but progressive noncompliance: things just kept getting more difficult until I was willing to draw the conclusions and go on to something else.

Time was getting short, also. By the end of September, most of the families who wintered outside of Barouk had left the village. October 1 is generally the beginning of the school year in Lebanon, so only those without school-age children and the full-time residents remained. Many of the latter were busy with the apple harvest and with buying and/or preserving the next year's food supply. I also was more pressed, since I had accepted a teaching job at the American University of Beirut three days a week.

Thus, even though only 55% of village households had been contacted (149 accepting and 40 rejecting participation), I decided to choose a sample and do the experiment before reserves of village cooperation and free time ran out. Those people with whom I had good personal relations could be asked to participate: they all had been interviewed and would provide conscientious cooperation and straight answers. Furthermore, the accuracy to which the informant sample represented the village population could be checked after interview responses had been fully analyzed. The problem thus became one of how many and which persons to choose. Accordingly, I searched for a local institution which could provide a model for such a sample, i.e., an institution broadly representative of groups in the village. The one which seemed to approximate this goal most closely was the former municipal council (Ar. *majlis 'al-baladīya*).

As was indicated earlier, this council was originally composed of twelve men chosen in 1964 by a popular election in Barouk and the neighboring hamlet of Fraydis.[1] According to local custom, eight of the council members –five Druzes and three Christians–represented Barouk, their official place of residence.[2] I was told the rationale behind this ratio was that in Barouk there were five Druze registered voters for every three Christian ones. The registration records for the (national) election in 1972 show 201 Druze households and 140 Christian ones, giving a ratio of 5:3.5. Analysis of the questionnaire data shows that the size of Christian and Druze households are nearly the same (6.2 and 6.4 members, respectively). Since the household

[1] Following the death of its chairman, the council split on election of his successor. The district administrator (*qa'imaqām*) dissolved it in December, 1973, and is currently responsible for the business formerly handled by it.

[2] The remaining four members–three Christians and one Druze, again apportioned according to local custom–represented Fraydis. Thus the total council was evenly balanced in terms of sect, with six Druze and six Christian members.

sizes are nearly the same, and the ratio of Druze to Christian households is substantially the same as that of the sects on the municipal council, I chose a sample of five Druzes and three Christians.

However, the municipal council did not provide an accurate model for factional divisions. As mentioned earlier, the Yazbaki faction has consistently dominated this council by winning the majority of its seats in every election held to date. In national politics, however, the reverse prevails: the Junblāṭṭi list has gotten a plurality in every election since 1957. Because Yazbakis win local elections, Junblāṭṭis national ones, it seemed most logical to choose a sample evenly divided between the factions, so that the five Druzes and three Christians were also evenly divided between Yazbakis and Junblāṭṭis.

Whether the municipal council provides an adequate model of village class structure is a more complicated question. In terms of the traditional classes, it does: of the twelve-member council, one (8.5%) was a šayk̠; registration records indicate that 26 (7.6%) of the 341 households belonged to the mušāyik̠ class. However, the traditional division of society into sheiks and commoners seems inadequate to account for present stratification in the village, as was discussed in Section 2. Briefly stated, some commoners have gone up and some sheiks have gone down. Mobility is shown in customs like the extension of deference behavior and titles indicating superior social status,[3] which formerly were associated only with sheiks, to some members of commoner families who have gained wealth and/or influence outside the village. It is shown in the growing number of marriages by sheikly sons and even daughters to persons who are not sheiks, and sometimes not even Druzes. It is shown in the funeral dispute, where commoners forced sheiks to adopt the same code of attendance and place in the procession of mourners to the burial place. It is shown in the increased status of Christians, taken as a group, relative to Druzes, as a group. Most generally, it is shown in the progressive replacement of status based on birth with that based on income, land ownership, education, work, and influence with centers of power outside the village. Thus, social mobility has not only meant a change of personnel, but also a change in the basis of class membership.

As the discussion in Section 2 shows, the households of Barouk can be categorized at present into three socio-economic classes. The "upper" class is constituted by 12 households or approximately 8% of the population interviewed; the "middle" class, by 39 households or 27% of that population;

[3]The titles were "šayk̠" (pl. "mušāyik̠") and/or "bayk" (pl. "bakawāt"). Notice that these titles indicate social status: Druze religious specialists are also called "mušāyik̠," but whenever it was necessary to be precise about the referent of the term, Baroukis marked religious referents by the expression mušāyik̠ 'ad-dīn ("the sheiks of religion").

and the "lower" class, by 95 households or 65% of that population. Accordingly, the informant sample for the psycholinguistic experiment should contain one member from the first group, two from the second, and five from the third. Since the questionnaire data had not yet been analyzed when the informants were selected, however, the "upper" class was overly represented in the sample actually chosen. Two members of that class participated in the experiment, as did two members of the "middle" class and four members of the "lower" one. This disadvantage in proportional representation of classes is somewhat offset by the advantage of including informants which better indicated the variations within the "upper" group: the two men chosen differed in terms of sect (Druze versus Maronite Christian) and traditional class background (sheik versus commoner). In short, the informant sample reflects the basic three-class system in the village, but it does so in such a way as to exaggerate somewhat the numerical proportion of the "upper" class vis-a-vis the others and to reflect variations within it.

Finally, something should be said about the sex and ages of the members of the sample. All the informants in the psycholinguistic experiment were male. There were two major reasons for this. First was the methodological one: the experiment, as we will see in a moment, is best performed by a single informant working with the experimenter in a fairly quiet place without major distractions. In the village of Barouk, as among probably most Middle Eastern societies, it is highly discouraged for a woman to be alone with a man who is neither her husband nor a member of her family. This problem, however, is not insurmountable.[4] Had it been necessary, I could have done the experiment during a visit accompanied by my ex-wife or asked her or another woman to administer it. This did not seem necessary because of the second reason. As was mentioned in Section 2, voting returns for national elections are subdivided into six groups: one group for men and one for women in each of the three wards of the village. So group 1 (men) and group 4 (women) are in one ward, groups 2 and 5 in another, and groups 3 and 6 in the last. The men's and women's returns in each ward appear to be highly correlated, as shown by Figure 9 (candidates Y and Z were on the same ticket).

Whether men follow the lead of women, or vice-versa, is not significant here. (The Baroukis I asked about this said that women generally vote as men advise them to.) What is significant is the apparent correlation between the two sets of data: knowing one, it seems possible to predict the other with a high degree of accuracy. Since each set of voting patterns was predictable from the other, it is reasonable to infer–in this ethnographic case–

---

[4] Figuratively speaking.

Figure 9[1]
Selected Voting Returns by Wards

	Voters' Group 1	Voters' Group 2	Voters' Group 3	Voters' Group 4	Voters' Group 5	Voters' Group 6
Candidate X	70	77	26	23	13	11
Candidate Y	18	13	39	39	45	40
Candidate Z	12	10	35	38	42	49
Totals	100	100	100	100	100	100
N	256	220	324	253	352	332

[1]These data were adapted from the returns for the 1972 national election.

that women's concepts about politics ought also to be predictable from men's.[5] Given this predictability, and because it was easier for me to do the experiment with males, only men were chosen for the sample.

The ages of these men ranged from 35 to 80 and each of them was head of his respective household. On the basis of the relative differences in their ages, they can be categorized into three "subgroups:" younger (35, 36), middle-aged (45, 50, 51), and older (60, 65, 80).

Having thus explained how the sample of informants was chosen for the psycholinguistic experiment, it is now appropriate to discuss how the terms under investigation were selected.

CHOICE OF TERMS

The examples of wāsiṭa presented in Sections 1 and 2 can now be reconsidered at a more abstract level. These examples show that every wāsiṭa is a transaction between three parties: an intermediating party (the wāsiṭa-maker) and the two parties he or she connects. Since the intermediating party may have entirely different kinds of relations with the other two, this triad resolves into two dyadic relationships: one between the intermediary and one party (who may have requested the wāsiṭa), and one between the intermediary and the other party (who is the target of the wāsiṭa). For instance, in the case of the transaction which brought a job to his son, Abu Fu'ad said that the "credit" (Ar. faḍl) for success went to his zaʿīm (the intermediary), not to the minister who actually supplied the job. Abu Fu'ad thus became obligated to the zaʿīm for interceding on his

[5]Of course, concepts are only one factor influencing behavior. The whole question of the fit, or lack of fit, between women's and men's actions and concepts about politics in Lebanon (and elsewhere) is certainly one which can and should be studied by more field research.

behalf, while the zaʿīm became obligated to the minister for providing the service. This minister will probably ask the zaʿīm to reciprocate at some future time in a matter having nothing to do with Abu Fu'ad.

The basic dyads in wāsiṭa transactions may be constituted by persons who have mutual or power relations with each other. Since the minister and the zaʿīm can supply each other with culturally equivalent rewards, they have a mutual relationship between equals, wherein each has only influence (Ar. *ta'sīr*) over the other. However, a mutual relationship is but one of the possible outcomes of social exchange; the other, according to Blau, is a power relationship. The links between the zaʿim and Abu Fu'ad exemplify such a tie, because Abu Fu'ad cannot supply rewards which are culturally equivalent to those provided by his zaʿīm. Thus, their relationship is an asymmetrical one between unequals, wherein the zaʿīm has power (Ar. *nufūz*) over Abu Fu'ad. The types of relations involved in a given transaction are clearly indicated by whether or not the intermediary's efforts can be refused by one or both of the other parties. For example, Faruq showed that he had a mutual relationship with Yusif when he refused to allow Yusif to mediate the dispute with Abu Karim. Abu Karim, on the other hand, had to accept Yusif's offer because of his subordinate status in their power relationship. Any particular wāsiṭa transaction, then, will manifest some permutation of these basic elements: a mutual-mutual transaction, a mutual-power one, etc.

This more abstract view of wāsita indicates how one might study what Baroukis think about the process. Since wāsiṭa is a transaction, it might be compared and contrasted with other transactional processes to show how it is similar to, and different from, them. For instance, the sample of Barouki informants discussed above could be given a set of cards bearing the Arabic names of different processes, including wāsiṭa, and asked to sort these cards into piles on the basis of similarities in the meanings they have. Then, if more informants sorted the wāsiṭa card with one glossed, say, as "leadership" than they did with one glossed as "friendship," the conclusion would be that for this group of native speakers the meaning of wāsiṭa was more like that of "leadership" than it was like that of "friendship."

This approach to the problem, however, is hampered by the small number of terms designating transactional processes in the daily speech of Baroukis. The paucity of terms designating processes contrasts sharply with the profusion of terms for statuses derived from their operation. For example, although I did not hear a term which might be glossed as "clientship," I often did hear words for "clients:" *'atbāʿ, zbunāt, zilm, maḥāsib,* etc. To refer to the processes, Baroukis would say *'illi byaʿmil 'al-X* ("what an X does"–"X" being a status term). This difference in lexical specialization presents intriguing semantic problems both within and between languages–

as the Sapir-Whorf hypothesis and myriad commentaries on it attest–but it is not directly germane to the research problem at hand.

Nevertheless, one can follow the lead of these native speakers in an interesting way. We have seen that wāsiṭa can be used as a reward traded in social exchange to establish and/or maintain relationships between parties considered to be equal in status or relationships between superiors and subordinates. The person who intermediates, "who does the wāsiṭa," is called a *wasīṭ*. Therefore, one can investigate whether a certain wasīṭ is considered to be more like a friend, relative, or neighbor–all roughly equal statuses in this village context–while another wasīṭ is considered to be more similar to a patron, broker, or leader–all apparently superior statuses in this village context. That is, each Arabic name of a status, and a sentence illustrating its relevant meaning, can be written on a card. Two separate cards, one card for each of its relevant meanings, will carry the name wasīṭ. Then the whole set of cards can be given to informants, who will sort them into piles according to similarities in meanings for the terms written on them. If the informants do in fact sort the relevant wasīṭ card with others carrying names of mutual statuses, and the second wasīṭ card with others carrying names of superior statuses, then it seems plausible to conclude that they conceive of wāsiṭa as a process which can be used to establish either mutual or power relationships. Conversely, if informants sort the two wasīṭ cards together into the same pile, then they conceive of no significant differences in meaning between a wāsiṭa used to establish a mutual relationship and a wāsiṭa used to establish a power relationship. Such a result would not necessarily disconfirm the analysis of wāsiṭa according to the social-exchange model, which seems to account for other behavior such as visiting patterns, informants' descriptions of behavior, etc. It would, however, indicate that local informants have a different view of the process. This, in turn, would require an explanation of why sorting behavior (and the conceptual structures implied by it) differs from other behavior observed in daily interactions and discussed in Sections 1 and 2.

Terms were chosen, then, according to several criteria. First, they had to be in use in the daily speech of Baroukis. Second, they should designate a broad range of mutual, superior, and subordinate statuses connected with economic, political, and social domains of activity. Third, they should cover intensively those statuses which both the present research and prior studies had emphasized as crucial in Lebanese village social structure. A list of the 18 terms chosen, and English glosses for them, appears in Figure 10.

A set of terms was thus selected for investigation. Earlier, the process of selecting the sample of informants was explained. It is now necessary to discuss how the two were combined–i.e., how the terms were presented to the sample of informants.

Figure 10
List of Arabic Terms Chosen for the Psycholinguistic Experiment

Term	English Gloss
1. ṣāḥib	"friend"
2. zbūn	"customer"
3. 'amīl	"agent"
4. wasīṭ	"(mutual) intermediary"
5. sayyid	"lord"
6. jār	"neighbor"
7. mu'allim	"master" (as in "master builder")
8. za'īm	"leader, political boss"
9. qabaḍay	"henchman"
10. simsār	"broker"
11. miftāḥ 'intikāb	"ward heeler"
12. maḥsūb	"protege"
13. tabi'	"follower"
14. wakīl	"representative"
15. zalami	"client"
16. wasīṭ	"(power) intermediary"
17. qarayib	"relative, kinsman"
18. ṣāḥib	"owner, possessor"

MANNER OF PRESENTATION OF TERMS TO INFORMANTS

In a pair of articles (1967, 1969), G. A. Miller has proposed a set of techniques for investigating how speakers of a language conceive of relations among the meanings associated with its terms. Following the procedures described in these articles, each of the statuses under study was written in Lebanese Colloquial Arabic, using Classical Arabic script,[6] on a four-by-six-inch file card in red ink. Then a sentence containing the term and illustrating the designative sense of meaning under study was written below in black ink, with the term of study underlined. When several senses of meanings associated with a term were under study (as was the case with wasīṭ and ṣāḥib), each sense was expressed on a separate card. For example, the "mutual" and "power" senses of wasīṭ were indicated by two different cards bearing the following sentences:

[6]This is the standard practice whenever Colloquial Arabic words must be written, e.g., in a newspaper or comic book.

(card 4)

بعض الناس بيقولوا أنه لازم الواحد يساعد
الوسيط الذي عم بيحل مشكلة بين شخصين بعائلته.

("Some people say that one must help the intermediary who is resolving a problem between two persons in his family.")

(card 16)

بعض الناس بيقولوا أنه لازم الواحد يساعد
الوسيط الذي بيخدمه بالشركات أو بالحكومة.

("Some people say that one must help the intermediary who is providing him services with companies or the government.")

All cards were then randomly ordered and given identification numbers for ease in recording results.

The experiment was administered to one informant at a time, generally during a visit to his home. Each informant was given the following explanation in Colloquial Arabic:

> Many people other than myself have done research on the economic, political, and social life in Lebanon, and to talk about that life they used several important expressions. I have noticed that Baroukis use some of these words and I would like to know how they think about them. So I thought I would ask a few people I know here if they could help me with this matter. I have written each of these expressions on a card in Colloquial Arabic (showing a card as example), and then I put the expression in a sentence underneath to show its meaning. When a word has more than one meaning (showing the cards for ṣāḥib), I put each meaning on a different card. For example, what does the word "ṣāḥib" mean on this card? (After the informant indicated it meant "friend," I went on.) And what does it mean here? (When he indicated it meant "owner, possessor," I continued.) Now I would like you to read all the cards and group them into piles according to their similarity of meaning. Make the comparison according to the language you speak at home with friends and family. For example,

> when the meaning of the word on this card is like the meaning of the word on that card, in your opinion, you put the cards together. When they are different, in your opinion, you put them in different piles. You can make as many piles, or put as many cards in each pile, as you want. Okay? When you finish I will ask you what is the meaning shared by all the cards in each pile.

When the informant had finished the task, the identification numbers of the cards in each pile were recorded on a separate sheet. Then the informant was asked if he could verbalize the meaning which the cards in each pile shared. When he could, this verbalization was written in the space following the list of numbers representing the appropriate pile. This set of results constituted the informant's "free sorts," i.e., those he had made only on the basis of similarity of meaning, as he conceived of it.

Next I told the informant the following:

> Now I would like to do something a little different. Last time you gave me the piles of cards which had similar meanings. This time I will tell you a meaning and I want you to give me all the cards which have that meaning. For example, look through the cards again and give me all those which refer to "persons between whom there is economic exchange" (Ar. *'ašḵāṣ fī baynathom mubādali iqtiṣadīya*).

When the informant presented all those cards, I asked him to indicate which of them referred to persons who had "higher status" (Ar. *markaz 'a'lā*) and which referred to persons who had "lower status" (Ar. *markaz 'awṭā*). When he completed that task, I recorded the results. Then I returned the cards to the deck, shuffled it, and gave all the cards back to the informant while asking for "persons between whom there is political exchange" (Ar. *'ašḵāṣ fī baynathom mubādali siyasīya*). When he gave me those cards, I again asked for "higher" and "lower" statuses, recorded the results, and mixed the cards back into the deck. Last, I asked the informant to give me all those cards referring to "persons between whom there is mutual social exchange" (Ar. *'ašḵāṣ fī baynathom mutabādali 'ijtima'īya*). When they were furnished, I noted the results and then mixed the cards back into the deck. Of course, this time I did not ask for "higher" or "lower" distinctions, since I had specifically requested "mutual" social exchange statuses before. This series of results constituted the informant's "fixed sorts," i.e., those made according to the criteria I specified.

In summary, cards carrying the terms to be investigated were composed according to the procedures described. Then these cards were given to the sample of informants, who sorted them as follows: first, on the basis of similarity of meaning, as they conceived of it; and second, on the basis of meanings I supplied. The analysis of the results of these techniques will be discussed in the next section.

ANALYSIS OF EXPERIMENTAL RESULTS

Free Sorts

After the experiment had been administered to all eight informants, their free-sort results were analyzed following the procedures specified by Miller (1967, 1969) and Johnson (1967). First, their result sheets were collated in a symmetric matrix for the 18 expressions under study (see Fig. 11). That is, each time an informant had put two terms in the same pile, a mark was placed in the matrix entry for their intersection. Marking the results from all eight informants produced a measurement of how "similar in meaning" the whole sample had considered the 18 items. This measurement was based on the assumption that the more informants who had grouped any two terms together, the more closely related were the terms' meanings and thus the higher was the terms' similarity value.

Drawing diagrams to indicate how the informants had grouped the meanings (and, therefore, how the meanings were related to one another) was the next step. Following Johnson's (1967) "hierarchical clustering schemes," two kinds of diagrams were drawn (see Fig. 12). The diagram on the left side (drawn by the "Connectedness" method)[7] shows how a given meaning was related to the most basic (or the most similar) clusters according to the largest value of similarity it had with at least one member of each of them. For example, $jār_6$ ("neighbor") has its largest similarity value, 4, with $qarayib_{17}$ ("relative, kinsman") because more informants (4) grouped these two items together than they grouped either of them with any other term—except one. $Ṣāḥib_1$ ("friend") also has a similarity value of 4 with $qarayib_{17}$, but it has only a value of 2 with $jār_6$. According to the Connectedness method, then, $ṣāḥib_1$ joins the cluster ($jār_6$, $qarayib_{17}$) at similarity value 4, its largest value with any member of the cluster. Conversely, the diagram on the right side of Figure 12 (drawn by the "Diameter" method) shows how terms were related according to the smallest value of similarity they have with any member of a cluster.[8] By the Diameter method, then, $ṣāḥib_1$ joins the cluster ($jār_6$, $qarayib_{17}$) at similarity value 2.

Now a question one can surely ask about these "schemes" is why not make the basic cluster in this case ($ṣāḥib_1$, $qarayib_{17}$) with $jār_6$ joining at a similarity value of 2, rather than the procedure described above. Both "basic" clusters are logical possibilities, so how should one choose between them? In this case, and throughout the analysis when a similar situation arose, the alternative taken was that which followed the informants' choices most closely. For this particular example, three informants actually made

---

[7]Johnson's terms for the two methods of diagramming clusters ("Connectedness" and "Diameter") correspond to Sokal and Sneath's "Single Linkage" and "Complete Linkage" methods, respectively (Sokal and Sneath 1963:180-83).

[8]Putting the more conservative picture on the right seems only fitting.

Figure 11
Similarity Matrix for Free Sorts

	1	2	3	4	5	6	7	8	9	10	11	12	13	14	15	16	17	18
1				2		2	2					1	1	1	1	1	4	
2			7	1	1				1	3		2	1	1	1	1		
3				1	1				1	4		2	1		1	1		
4					1	2				1						2	3	1
5							2	7	2		2					3		
6							1					1				1	4	2
7								2				2	1	2	1	2	1	1
8									3		2					3		
9										1	3	4	4		5	2		
10											1	2	1	1	1	2		
11												2	1		2	1		
12													3	1	5	2	1	
13														1	5	1		
14															1		1	1
15																1		
16																	1	
17																		1
18																		

Figure 12
Free-Sort Diagrams
(Nodes Common to the Two Diagrams are Circled)

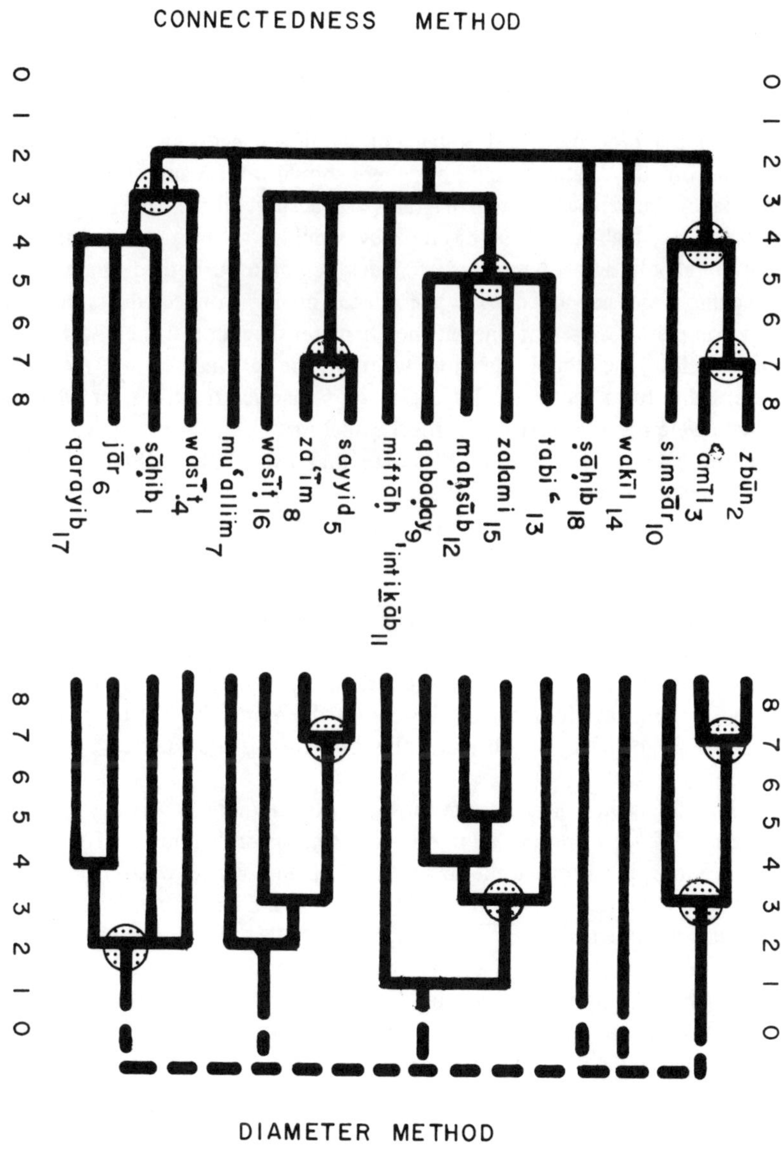

a two-member cluster of (jār$_6$, qarayib$_{17}$), while only one made the alternative, so the former cluster was taken as the basic one. Adding this principle to the clustering "schemes" thus clarifies possibly ambiguous readings of the similarity matrix.

Johnson explains how it may be possible to make a single value of similarity by averaging the values which an item has with the different members of a cluster, but he advises against using such a method. Rather, he stresses the utility of having two explicit hierarchical diagrams as a check on the results of the procedure. Although one would expect a more conservative picture from the Diameter method, there should not be an extremely large discrepancy between the two diagrams, especially at the larger values of similarity. A high degree of discrepancy would be shown, for instance, if there were only a small number of nodes common to both diagrams or if a meaning were associated with one cluster on the Connectedness diagram but a completely different one on the Diameter diagram. If there were such discrepancies, one could question whether the original set of meanings actually did form hierarchically organized semantic structures, or whether the data were not too "noisy" for precise analysis.

In the case at hand, Figure 12 shows that five of the eight clusters on the Connectedness diagram correspond to five of eleven on the Diameter diagram. (The dashed lines in the diagram on the right indicate the sorts of clustering one would expect to find, according to the diagram on the left, if the informant sample had been larger.) While the Connectedness method tends to maximize the values of all "mixed" relationships, the Diameter method does the opposite, i.e., to minimize them. The discrepancy evident between the two diagrams, therefore, seems to be a product simply of the greater number of clusters on the more conservative Diameter diagram. A good way of checking this inference is provided by the fixed-sort results.

Before discussing those results, however, let us note in passing that the two senses of wasīṭ are located in different clusters on Figure 12. The difference is more apparent in the Diameter diagram, where wasīṭ$_{16}$ ("power intermediary") is grouped with *sayyid*$_5$, zaʿīm$_8$, and *muʿallim*$_7$; while wasīṭ$_4$ ("mutual intermediary") is grouped with ṣāḥib$_1$, jār$_6$, and qarayib$_{17}$. According to the free-sort diagrams, therefore, the two senses of wasīṭ were seen to be more similar in meaning to other terms than they were to each other. The precise features of meaning each sense of wasīṭ shares with those other terms will be examined during discussion of the fixed-sort results.

Fixed Sorts

Whereas during the free sorts informants were grouping terms according to what they conceived to be similarities in meanings, during the fixed sorts they were supplying the terms associated with semantic categories specified by the experimenter. Those categories—"persons between whom there is economic exchange," "persons between whom there is political exchange," and "persons between whom there is mutual social exchange," as well as the subordinate categories of "higher statuses" and "lower statuses"—were predictions derived from the social-exchange model developed earlier in this monograph to explain the wāsiṭa process.

Notice that the free-sort data had *not* been analyzed prior to doing the fixed sorts: Johnson's "hierarchical clustering schemes" operate on the summed totals of all informants' clusters, compiled after the whole sample have finished the experiment. Now that free sorts *have* been analyzed, however, a comparison of both kinds of sorts is possible. The Cochran's Q test can be used to show whether any difference between them is significant at the .05 level. This statistical test compares fixed-sort results for a given semantic category with the relevant free-sort results, as shown by the more conservative Diameter diagram. The null hypothesis, H_O, is that there is no significant difference between the two kinds of sorts; only in the case shown on Figure 13 is the actual variation large enough to reject H_O. That is, in this case alone—which concerns "persons between whom there is economic exchange"—the difference between fixed-sort and free-sort results is so large that it could occur by chance only five times out of a hundred. In contrast, Figures 14 and 15 show that the variation between fixed-sort and free-sort results for both "persons . . . political exchange" and "persons . . . mutual social exchange" is so small that H_O cannot be rejected. Thus there are good statistical reasons for making two general conclusions. The first is that predictions derived from the social-exchange model of wāsiṭa regarding "persons . . . political exchange" and "persons . . . mutual social exchange" correspond to conceptual categories actually held by the sample of Barouki informants as a whole. The second is that these two categories contain the meanings associated with the terms clustered together in each sorting task.[9]

Both of these conclusions have further implications.

First, if these categories contain the meanings clustered in each group, do they not provide a labeling for the higher nodes on the free-sort diagram? That is, are not the fixed-sort categories actually the superordinates for meanings clustered beneath them, as "tree" is a semantic superordinate

[9] In her analysis of the same data, C. D. Miller (1978) has found corroborating results by a different method, multidimensional scaling.

Figure 13
Cochran's Q Test for Significant Difference between All Subjects' Fixed Sorts and Their Analyzed Free Sorts (as shown by the diameter diagram) for "Persons between Whom There is Economic Exchange"

Card Number	Fixed Sorts 1	2	3	4	5	6	7	8	Free Sorts	L_i	L_i^2
1.	0	0	0	0	0	0	0	0	0	0	0
2.	1	1	1	1	1	1	1	1	1	9	81
3.	1	1	1	1	1	1	1	1	1	9	81
4.	0	1	0	0	0	0	0	0	0	1	1
5	0	0	0	0	0	1	0	0	0	1	1
6.	0	0	0	0	0	0	0	1	0	1	1
7.	0	0	0	1	0	0	0	1	0	2	4
8.	0	0	0	0	0	1	0	0	0	1	1
9.	0	0	0	0	1	1	0	0	0	2	4
10.	1	1	1	1	1	1	1	0	1	8	64
11.	0	0	0	0	0	1	0	0	0	1	1
12.	0	0	1	0	1	0	0	0	0	2	4
13.	0	0	0	0	1	1	0	0	0	2	4
14.	0	0	0	1	1	1	1	1	0	5	25.
15.	0	0	0	0	1	1	0	0	0	2	4
16.	0	1	0	0	1	1	0	1	0	4	16
17.	0	0	0	0	0	0	0	0	0	0	0
18.	0	0	0	1	1	0	0	1	0	3	9
	3	5	4	6	10	11	4	7	3	53	301

$\Sigma Gj = 53$

$$Q = (9\text{-}1) \frac{(9\ [3^2+5^2+4^2+6^2+10^2+11^2+4^2+7^2+3^2]\ \text{-}53^2)}{9(53)\text{-}301} = 28.18$$

H_o = no significant difference between all subjects' fixed sorts and their analyzed free sorts

df = 9-1 = 8
$p(\chi^2 \geqslant 15.51) = .05$
$28.18 > 15.51$

Therefore, H_o *can* be rejected.

Figure 14
Cochran's Q Test for Significant Difference between All Subjects' Fixed Sorts and Their Analyzed Free Sorts (as shown by the diameter diagram) for "Persons between Whom There is Political Exchange"

Card Number	Fixed Sorts 1	2	3	4	5	6	7	8	Free Sorts	L_i	L_i^2
1.	0	0	0	0	0	0	0	1	0	1	1
2.	0	0	0	0	1	0	0	0	0	1	1
3.	0	0	0	0	1	1	0	0	0	2	4
4.	0	0	0	0	0	0	0	1	0	1	1
5.	1	1	1	1	1	1	1	1	1	9	81
6.	0	0	0	0	0	0	0	0	0	0	0
7.	1	1	1	0	0	1	0	1	1	6	36
8.	1	1	1	1	1	1	1	1	1	9	81
9.	1	1	1	1	1	0	1	0	1	7	49
10.	0	0	0	0	1	0	0	0	0	1	1
11.	1	1	1	1	1	1	0	1	1	8	64
12.	1	0	1	1	1	1	1	0	1	7	49
13.	1	0	1	1	1	1	0	1	1	7	49
14.	0	0	0	0	0	0	0	0	0	0	0
15.	1	1	1	1	1	1	1	0	1	8	64
16.	1	0	1	1	0	0	0	0	1	4	16
17.	0	0	0	0	0	0	0	1	0	1	1
18.	0	0	0	0	0	0	0	0	0	0	0
	9	6	9	8	10	8	5	8	9	72	498

Σ Gj = 72

$$Q = (9\text{-}1) \frac{(9\ [9^2+6^2+9^2+8^2+10^2+8^2+5^2+8^2+9^2]\ -72^2)}{9(72)\text{-}498} = 9.60$$

H_O = no significant difference between all subjects' fixed sorts and their analyzed free sorts

df = 9-1 = 8
$p(\chi^2 \geqslant 15.51) = .05$
$9.60 < 15.51$

Therefore, H_O *cannot* be rejected.

Figure 15
Cochran's Q Test for Significant Difference between All Subjects' Fixed Sorts and Their Analyzed Free Sorts (as shown by the diameter diagram) for "Persons between Whom There is Mutual Social Exchange"

Card Number	Fixed Sorts 1	2	3	4	5	6	7	8	Free Sorts	L_i	L_i^2
1.	1	1	1	1	1	1	1	1	1	9	81
2.	0	0	0	0	0	0	0	0	0	0	0
3.	0	0	0	0	0	0	0	0	0	0	0
4.	1	0	1	1	0	1	1	0	1	6	36
5.	0	0	0	0	1	0	0	0	0	1	1
6.	0	1	1	1	1	0	1	1	1	7	49
7.	0	0	0	0	1	0	0	0	0	1	1
8.	0	0	0	0	1	0	0	0	0	1	1
9.	0	0	0	0	0	0	0	0	0	0	0
10.	0	0	0	0	0	0	0	0	0	0	0
11.	0	0	0	0	0	1	0	0	0	1	1
12.	0	0	0	0	0	0	0	0	0	0	0
13.	0	0	0	0	0	0	0	0	0	0	0
14.	0	0	0	0	0	1	0	0	0	1	1
15.	0	0	0	0	1	0	0	0	0	1	1
16.	0	0	0	0	0	0	0	0	0	0	0
17.	1	1	1	1	1	1	1	1	1	9	81
18.	0	1	1	0	0	1	0	0	0	3	9
	3	4	5	4	7	6	4	3	4	40	262

Σ Gj = 40

$$Q = (9\text{-}1)\ \frac{(9\,[3^2+4^2+5^2+4^2+7^2+6^2+4^2+3^2+4^2]\ \text{-}40^2)}{9(40)\text{-}262} = 10.45$$

H_o = no significant difference between all subjects' fixed sorts and their analyzed free sorts

df = 9-1 = 8
$p(\chi^2 \geqslant 15.51) = .05$
$10.45 < 15.51$

Therefore, H_o *cannot* be rejected.

for "white oak," "red maple," "hickory," etc? If so, can't this insight be used to help label all the nodes on the free-sort taxonomy?

Second, if there are good statistical reasons for concluding that the above predictions are "psychologically real" for the whole sample of informants, does it follow that the same is true for the different subgroups constituting that sample? Or is it the case that the members of the various subgroups differ significantly in the ways they conceive of the semantic relations concerned? If the latter, can one show that different subgroups have different linguistic styles, or "codes," as ethnographers of communication (like Bernstein, Hymes, and Gumperz) have claimed?

The answer to most of these rhetorical questions is a clear "yes." The following discussion will seek to explain why, taking the two sets of implications in order.

The first set of implications concerns labeling semantic categories. Remember that fixed-sort results were gathered before the free-sort ones had been analyzed. Because of the ways informants conceived of the semantic relationships involved, however, the same meanings were clustered in the same ways in both sets of data. One set was obtained from the "bottom up"; free-sort meanings were grouped together on the basis of shared semantic features. The other set of data was obtained from the "top down"; fixed-sort results were produced when semantic categories were specified and those meanings included in their classes were sorted out. The substantial matching of semantic superordinates and subordinates was obtained for two of the three categories specified. However, Figures 16, 17, 18, and 19 show that this matching is even stronger for "second level" superordinates: within the "persons . . . economic exchange" category, there is significant difference between fixed-sort and free-sort results for "lower statuses" but *not* for "higher statuses"; while within the "persons . . . political exchange" category, there is no significant difference between the two kinds of sorts for either "higher" or "lower" statuses. In other words, the matching is good even for one of the subcategories of "persons . . . economic exchange," as well as for both subcategories of "persons . . . political exchange." This difference in variation between fixed-sort and free-sort results at "first-level" and "second-level" superordinates is an interesting point which will be investigated further during the discussion of subgroup variations.

Since two of the most abstract free-sort clusters have "psychological reality" for the sample of informants, it becomes worthwhile to attempt labeling the other clusters which occur in the diameter diagram. The informants' verbalizations about clusters they made provide useful first approximations to these other labels. Although such verbalizations are neither necessary (since some informants couldn't provide them for all

Figure 16
Cochran's Q Test for Significant Difference between All Subjects' Fixed Sorts and Their Analyzed Free Sorts (as shown by the diameter diagram) for "Higher Statuses" among "Persons between Whom There is Economic Exchange"

Card Number	Fixed Sorts 1	2	3	4	5	6	7	8	Free Sorts	L_i	L_i^2
1.	0	0	0	0	0	0	0	0	0	0	0
2.	0	0	0	0	0	0	0	1	0	1	1
3.	0	0	0	0	0	0	0	0	0	0	0
4.	0	1	0	0	0	0	0	0	0	1	1
5.	0	0	0	0	0	0	0	0	0	0	0
6.	0	0	0	0	0	0	0	0	0	0	0
7.	0	0	0	1	0	0	0	1	0	2	4
8.	0	0	0	0	0	0	0	0	0	0	0
9.	0	0	0	0	0	0	0	0	0	0	0
10.	1	1	0	0	0	0	1	0	1	4	16
11.	0	0	0	0	0	0	0	0	0	0	0
12.	0	0	0	0	0	0	0	0	0	0	0
13.	0	0	0	0	0	0	0	0	0	0	0
14.	0	0	0	0	0	0	1	0	0	1	1
15.	0	0	0	0	0	0	0	0	0	0	0
16.	0	1	0	0	0	0	0	0	0	1	1
17.	0	0	0	0	0	0	0	0	0	0	0
18.	0	0	0	1	0	0	0	0	0	1	1
	1	3	0	2	0	0	2	2	1	11	25

$\Sigma Gj = 11$

$$Q = (9\text{-}1)\ \frac{(9\ [1^2+3^2+0^2+2^2+0^2+0^2+2^2+2^2+1^2]\ -11^2)}{9(11)\text{-}25} = 9.30$$

H_o = no significant difference between all subjects' fixed sorts and their analyzed free sorts.

df = 9-1 = 8
$p(\chi^2 \geqslant 15.51) = .05$
$9.30 < 15.51$

Therefore, H_o *cannot* be rejected.

Figure 17
Cochran's Q Test for Significant Difference between All Subjects' Fixed Sorts and Their Analyzed Free Sorts (as shown by the diameter diagram) for "Lower Statuses" among "Persons between Whom There is Economic Exchange"

Card Number	Fixed Sorts 1	2	3	4	5	6	7	8	Free Sorts	L_i	L_i^2
1.	0	0	0	0	0	0	0	0	0	0	0
2.	1	1	0	1	0	0	1	0	1	5	25
3.	1	1	0	1	1	0	1	1	1	7	49
4.	0	0	0	0	0	0	0	0	0	0	0
5.	0	0	0	0	0	0	0	0	0	0	0
6.	0	0	0	0	0	0	0	0	0	0	0
7.	0	0	0	0	0	0	0	0	0	0	0
8.	0	0	0	0	0	0	0	0	0	0	0
9.	0	0	0	0	1	0	0	0	0	1	1
10.	0	0	0	1	0	0	0	0	0	1	1
11.	0	0	0	0	0	0	0	0	0	0	0
12.	0	0	0	0	1	0	0	0	0	1	1
13.	0	0	0	0	1	0	0	0	0	1	1
14.	0	0	0	1	0	0	0	0	0	1	1
15.	0	0	0	0	1	0	0	0	0	1	1
16.	0	0	0	0	1	0	0	0	0	1	1
17.	0	0	0	0	0	0	0	0	0	0	0
18.	0	0	0	0	0	0	0	0	0	0	0
	2	2	0	4	6	0	2	1	2	19	81

$\Sigma Gj = 19$

$$Q = (9\text{-}1) \frac{(9\ [2^2+2^2+0^2+4^2+6^2+0^2+2^2+1^2+2^2]\ \text{-}19^2)}{9(19)\text{-}81} = 23.11$$

H_o = no significant difference between all subjects' fixed sorts and their analyzed free sorts

df = 9-1 = 8
$p(\chi^2 \geqslant 15.51) = .05$
$23.11 > 15.51$

Therefore, H_o *can* be rejected.

Figure 18
Cochran's Q Test for Significant Difference between All Subjects' Fixed Sorts and Their Analyzed Free Sorts (as shown by the diameter diagram) for "Higher Statuses" among "Persons between Whom There is Political Exchange"

Card Number	Fixed Sorts 1	2	3	4	5	6	7	8	Free Sorts	L_i	L_i^2
1.	0	0	0	0	0	0	0	0	0	0	0
2.	0	0	0	0	0	0	0	0	0	0	0
3.	0	0	0	0	0	0	0	0	0	0	0
4.	0	0	0	0	0	0	0	0	0	0	0
5.	1	1	1	1	1	1	1	1	1	9	81
6.	0	0	0	0	0	0	0	0	0	0	0
7.	1	0	0	0	0	1	0	1	1	4	16
8.	1	1	1	1	1	1	1	1	1	9	81
9.	0	0	1	0	0	0	1	0	0	2	4
10.	0	0	0	0	0	0	0	0	0	0	0
11.	0	1	1	0	0	0	0	1	0	3	9
12.	0	0	0	0	0	0	0	0	0	0	0
13.	0	0	0	0	0	0	0	0	0	0	0
14.	0	0	0	0	0	0	0	0	0	0	0
15.	0	0	0	0	0	0	0	0	0	0	0
16.	1	0	1	1	0	0	0	0	1	4	16
17.	0	0	0	0	0	0	0	0	0	0	0
18.	0	0	0	0	0	0	0	0	0	0	0
	4	3	5	3	2	3	3	4	4	31	207

$\Sigma\, Gj = 31$

$$Q = (9\text{-}1)\ \frac{(9\ [4^2+3^2+5^2+3^2+2^2+3^2+3^2+4^2+4^2]\ \text{-}31^2)}{9(31)\text{-}207} = 6.22$$

H_o = no significant difference between all subjects' fixed sorts and their analyzed free sorts

df = 9-1 = 8
$p(\chi^2 \geqslant 15.51) = .05$
$6.22 < 15.51$

Therefore, H_o *cannot* be rejected.

Figure 19
Cochran's Q Test for Significant Difference between All Subjects' Fixed Sorts and Their Analyzed Free Sorts (as shown by the diameter diagram) for "Lower Statuses" among "Persons between Whom There is Political Exchange"

Card Number	Fixed Sorts 1	2	3	4	5	6	7	8	Free Sorts	L_i	L_i^2
1.	0	0	0	0	0	0	0	1	0	1	1
2.	0	0	0	0	0	0	0	0	0	0	0
3.	0	0	0	0	0	0	0	0	0	0	0
4.	0	0	0	0	0	0	0	1	0	1	1
5.	0	0	0	0	0	0	0	0	0	0	0
6.	0	0	0	0	0	0	0	0	0	0	0
7.	0	1	1	0	0	0	0	0	0	2	4
8.	0	0	0	0	0	0	0	0	0	0	0
9.	1	1	0	1	1	0	0	0	1	5	25
10.	0	0	0	0	0	0	0	0	0	0	0
11.	1	0	0	1	1	0	0	0	1	4	16
12.	1	0	1	1	1	1	1	0	1	7	49
13.	1	0	1	1	1	1	0	1	1	7	49
14.	0	0	0	0	0	0	0	0	0	0	0
15.	1	1	1	1	1	1	1	0	1	8	64
16.	0	0	0	0	0	0	0	0	0	0	0
17.	0	0	0	0	0	0	0	1	0	1	1
18.	0	0	0	0	0	0	0	0	0	0	0
	5	3	4	5	5	3	2	4	5	36	210

$\Sigma\, Gj = 36$

$$Q = (9\text{-}1)\ \frac{(9\,[5^2+3^2+4^2+5^2+5^2+3^2+2^2+4^2+5^2]\ \text{-}36^2)}{9(36)\text{-}210} = 6.32$$

H_o = no significant difference between all subjects' fixed sorts and their analyzed free sorts

df = 9-1 = 8
$p(\chi^2 \geqslant 15.51) = .05$
$6.32 < 15.51$

Therefore, H_o *cannot* be rejected.

clusters) nor sufficient (since not all the clusters on the Diameter diagram were actually made by informants), still they supply hints or clues towards hypotheses which one might propose. For example, one informant verbalized the cluster (jār$_6$, qarayib$_{17}$) as *'aṣ-ṣilat 'al-ḥatimīya* ("the unchangeable tie"). He also expressed the common meaning of the cluster (sayyid$_5$, za'īm$_8$) as *'aṣ-ṣilat 'al-qa'idīya* ("the leadership tie").

Colloquial Arabic dictionaires can provide another source of suggestions for labeling the clusters. Dictionary senses can be combined in a manner consistent with the neutralizations of semantic contrasts implied by the Diameter diagram. For instance, since *miftāḥ 'intikāb* literally means "an election key" (i.e., someone who can deliver a bloc of votes), a feature which can differentiate the meaning of this term from the others of the "lower, political exchange status" category might be a contextual specification: *'ikṭiyāri* ("electoral").

Notice that I am not claiming informant verbalizations or dictionary senses are either sufficient or even necessary to the process of labeling nodes. They are simply hints, clues toward hypotheses which might be tried. The informants' ability to cluster terms indicates that, at least on some level, they perceive some common feature(s) among the terms' meanings. Similarly, the dictionary senses of a term often cross-reference synonyms, which apparently share some feature(s) of meaning. The job of the analyst is to identify the feature(s). In this task he or she can use all the information available, and informant verbalizations and dictionary senses may well supply *some* of that. So also may the analyst's intuitive feel for the language, knowledge of linguistic theory and of the sociocultural environment in which the language is spoken, and so on. Whatever its sources, the labeling system has to meet the obvious formal criteria of consistency, sufficiency, and economy.

Attempting to incorporate all of these considerations, then, Figure 20 presents a tentative labeling of the clusters shown on the Diameter diagram. These labels, though tentative, provide a concise statement of the significant contrasts existing among the semantic structures displayed. Accordingly, they provide a unique specification for each meaning whether one reads either "up" or "down" the diagram. Going "up" (left to right) gives a listing of the most superficial to the most abstract features; going "down" (right to left), from the most general to the most particular classes. For example, wasīṭ$_{16}$ has the specification of "medial, higher, political exchange status;" while wasīṭ$_4$ carries one of a "medial, mutual social exchange status."

The second set of implications concerned possible differences in sorting related to the various subgroups composing the informant sample. During the discussion of how informants were chosen, we saw that members of the sample contrasted in terms of four dimensions: class, age, sect, and faction.

Figure 20
Tentative Labeling of Clusters on the Diameter Diagram

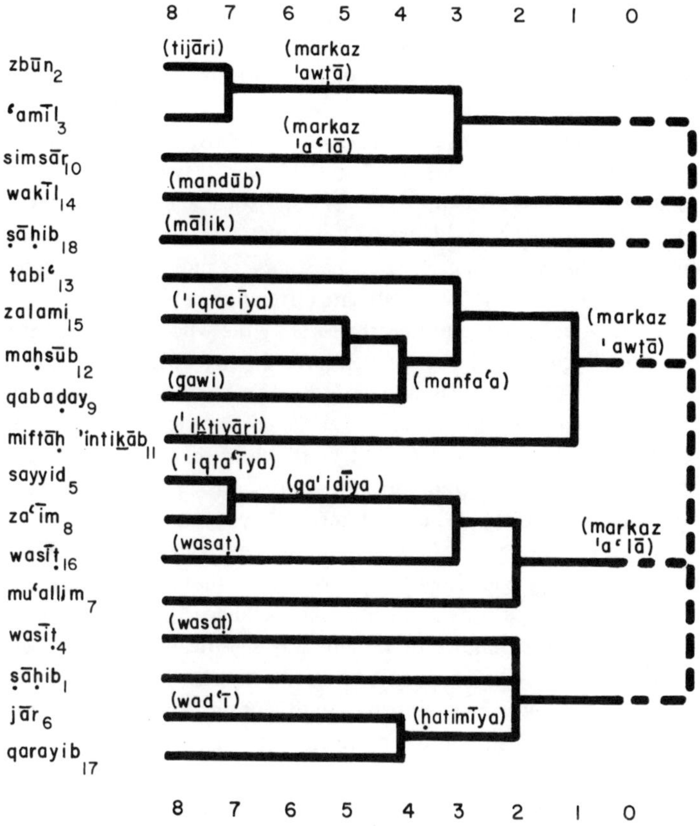

Figure 21
English Glosses for the Tentative Arabic Labels

Tentative Arabic Labels	English Glosses
1. markaz 'aʿlā	"higher status"
2. markaz 'awṭā	"lower status"
3. manfaʿa	"profit-seeking"
4. qa'idīya	"leadership"
5. ḥatimīya	"unchangeable"
6. tijāri	"commercial"
7. mandūb	"delegated"
8. mālik	"proprietary"
9. 'iqtaʿīya	"feudal"
10. qawi	"forceful"
11. 'ik̲tiyāri	"electoral"
12. wasaṭ	"medial"
13. wadʿī	"locative"

(The dimension of sex was also discussed but not considered distinctive in this case.) Taking each of these contrasts in order, we will now examine how well the fixed-sort results of the various subgroups matched the free-sort results of the whole sample of informants, thereby indicating how conceptual differences may be correlated with differences in subgroup membership.

In terms of the dimension of socio-economic class, the informant sample was divided into four members of Class I ("lower"), two of Class II ("middle"), and two of Class III ("upper"). The statistical analyses for these three subgroups are presented as Figures 22 through 28. For the categories of "persons . . . political exchange" and "persons . . . mutual social exchange" (Figs. 23 and 24), there is no significant difference between the fixed sorts by any of the three classes and the free sorts by the whole informant sample. Similarly, for "higher" and "lower" statuses among "persons . . . political exchange" (Figs. 26 and 27), none of the three classes shows significant difference between fixed sorts and free sorts. Since the major focus of this monograph is the wasiṭa process, it is worthwhile to emphasize that members of all three classes sorted the two wasīṭ cards as the social exchange model predicted: wasīṭ_{16} ("power intermediary") was placed in a pile for "higher statuses" among "persons . . . political exchange;" wasīṭ_4 ("mutual intermediary") was grouped with "persons . . . mutual social exchange."

For the category "persons . . . economic exchange," however, the picture is different. Figure 22 shows that there was significant variation between fixed sorts and free sorts for members of the upper class, but for neither the middle nor the lower one. For the subdivisions of this category, "higher" and "lower" statuses, the picture is more complex. For the former, Figure 25 shows that there was *no* significant variation for any of the three classes; for the latter, Figure 26 shows that there *was* significant variation for both upper and lower classes, but not for the middle one. Notice that the difference for the lower class is significant by only a small amount ($10.00 > 9.49$), while that for the upper class is more than four times larger. Actually the lower-class results would not have been statistically significant ($8.00 < 9.49$) if only one of their sorts were changed. Perhaps, then, we may be justified in considering these particular experimental results to be due to chance. Such a consideration would clarify the overall picture of differences in sorting for the two categories concerned. Earlier, the examination of sorts made by the whole sample of informants (Figs. 13 through 19) showed that significant difference occurred only in the cases of "persons . . . economic exchange" and its "lower status" subdivision. Now, the examination of sorts made by different classes shows that the only significant difference occurs with the same categories and overwhelmingly is due to the fixed sorts of the two upper-class informants. This is probably what one should expect:

given that these members of the upper class have Westernized, university-level educations and are employed as professionals in the national capital, it seems only natural that they would have more commercialized–some might say "modern"–conceptions of the meanings under study. Sir Henry Maine, to take an example, built a whole theory of social evolution on the progressive development of contractual ties between social actors. However, it is hardly necessary to adopt that orientation here; it suffices for present purposes to show that the conceptual differences are correlated with membership in the lower, middle, or upper class, which has been done.

In terms of the dimension of age, the sample was also divided into three subgroups: younger (ages 35 and 36), middle-aged (45, 50, 51), and older (60, 65, 80). Again, the only significant difference concerns the "persons . . . economic exchange" category and its "lower status" subdivision. Figures 29 and 33 show that, for these two categories, the younger subgroup's fixed sorts differed significantly from the free sorts of the whole informant sample, while neither the middle-aged or older subgroups' did. Again, also, there was no significant difference between fixed and free sorts by any of the age subgroups for any of the other semantic categories, as Figures 30, 31, 32, 34, and 35 attest.

The significant results for the younger subgroup indicate a problem of interpretation. Any reader who compares the fixed sorts of the younger subgroup (especially Figures 29 and 33) with those of the upper class (especially 22 and 26) will see that they are identical. That is, the two informants who were youngest were also the representatives of the upper class. This situation clearly illustrates the hazards of working with a small sample of informants: there is no way now to be sure whether these two informants' fixed sorts were due to their ages or class membership. Age may have been a factor. Changes in leader-follower relations from feudal to modern times were discussed in Section 2; and the youth club skit noted earlier indicated a difference between younger and older people's views of the current economic and political situation. Class may also have been a factor, for the variations in visiting behavior, marriage practices, and titles of respect were only three from many indications of possible differences in conceptions between classes. Therefore, it is plausible that both factors were involved, and an assaying of their relative importance awaits further research. Before going on, however, let us note that this problem does not concern the major focus of this monograph–the study of wāsiṭa–because there was no significant difference among either class or age subgroups in regard to how the two senses of wasīṭ were categorized.

In terms of the dimension of religious sect, the informant sample was divided into three Christians and five Druzes. The statistical analyses of sorts by these subgroups are given as Appendixes 2*a* through 2*i*. Again

Figure 22
Cochran's Q Test for Significant Difference between Lower (Class I), Middle (Class II), and Upper (Class III) Subgroups' Fixed Sorts and Their Analyzed Free Sorts (as shown by the diameter diagram) for "Persons between Whom There is Economic Exchange"

Card Number	Fixed Sorts I				Fixed Sorts II		Fixed Sorts III		Free Sorts	L_i I	L_i II	L_i III	L_i^2 I	L_i^2 II	L_i^2 III
1.	0	0	0	0	0	0	0	0	0	0	0	0	0	0	0
2.	1	1	1	1	1	1	1	1	1	5	3	3	25	9	9
3.	1	1	1	1	1	1	1	1	1	5	3	3	25	9	9
4.	1	0	0	0	0	0	0	0	0	1	0	0	1	0	0
5.	0	0	0	0	0	0	0	1	0	0	0	1	0	0	1
6.	0	0	0	0	1	0	0	0	0	0	1	0	0	1	0
7.	0	0	0	1	1	0	0	0	0	1	1	0	1	1	0
8.	0	0	0	0	0	0	0	1	0	0	0	1	0	0	1
9.	0	0	0	0	0	0	1	1	0	0	0	2	0	0	4
10.	1	1	1	1	0	1	1	1	1	5	2	3	25	4	9
11.	0	0	0	0	0	0	0	1	0	0	0	1	0	0	1
12.	0	0	1	0	0	0	1	0	0	1	0	1	1	0	1
13.	0	0	0	0	0	0	1	1	0	0	0	2	0	0	4
14.	0	0	0	1	1	1	1	1	0	1	2	2	1	4	4
15.	0	0	0	0	0	0	1	1	0	0	0	2	0	0	4
16.	1	0	0	0	1	0	1	1	0	1	1	2	1	1	4
17.	0	0	0	0	1	0	1	1	0	0	0	0	0	0	0
18.	0	0	0	1	1	0	1	0	0	1	1	1	1	1	1
	5	3	4	6	7	4	10	11	3	21	14	24	81	30	52

$\Sigma Gj_I = 21$ $\qquad$ $\Sigma Gj_{II} = 14$ $\qquad$ $\Sigma Gj_{III} = 24$

$$Q_I = (5\text{-}1)\ \frac{(5\ [5^2+3^2+4^2+6^2+3^2]\ -21^2)}{5(21)\text{-}81} = 5.67$$

$$Q_{II} = (3\text{-}1)\ \frac{(3\ [7^2+4^2+3^2]\ -14^2)}{3(14)\text{-}30} = 4.33$$

$$Q_{III} = (3\text{-}1)\ \frac{(3\ [10^2+11^2+3^2]\ -24^2)}{3(24)\text{-}52} = 11.40$$

H_o = no significant difference between lower, middle, and upper subgroups' fixed sorts and their analyzed free sorts

$df_I = 5\text{-}1 = 4$
$p(\chi^2 \geqslant 9.49) = .05$
$5.67 < 9.49$

$df_{II} = 3\text{-}1 = 2$
$p(\chi^2 \geqslant 5.99) = .05$
$4.33 < 5.99$

$df_{III} = 3\text{-}1 = 2$
$p(\chi^2 \geqslant 5.99) = .05$
$11.40 > 5.99$

Therefore H_o *can* be rejected for the upper subgroups but *not* for the lower or middle ones.

Figure 23
Cochran's Q Test for Significant Difference between Lower (Class I), Middle (Class II), and Upper (Class III) Subgroups' Fixed Sorts and Their Analyzed Free Sorts (as shown by the diameter diagram) for "Persons between Whom There is Political Exchange"

Card Number	Fixed Sorts I				Fixed Sorts II		Fixed Sorts III		Free Sorts	L_i I	L_i II	L_i III	L_i^2 I	L_i^2 II	L_i^2 III
1.	0	0	0	0	0	1	0	0	0	0	1	0	0	1	0
2.	0	0	0	0	0	0	1	0	0	0	0	1	0	0	1
3.	0	0	0	0	0	0	1	1	0	0	0	2	0	0	4
4.	0	0	0	0	0	1	0	0	0	0	1	0	0	1	0
5.	1	1	1	1	1	1	1	1	1	5	3	3	25	9	9
6.	0	0	0	0	0	0	0	0	0	0	0	0	0	0	0
7.	1	1	1	0	0	1	0	1	1	4	2	2	16	4	4
8.	1	1	1	1	1	1	1	1	1	5	3	3	25	9	9
9.	1	1	1	1	1	0	1	0	1	5	2	2	25	4	4
10.	0	0	0	0	0	0	1	0	0	0	0	1	0	0	1
11.	1	1	1	1	0	1	1	1	1	5	2	3	25	4	9
12.	1	0	1	1	1	0	1	1	1	4	2	3	16	4	9
13.	1	0	1	1	0	1	1	1	1	4	2	3	16	4	9
14.	0	0	0	0	0	0	0	0	0	0	0	0	0	0	0
15.	1	1	1	1	1	0	1	1	1	5	2	3	25	4	9
16.	1	0	1	1	0	0	0	0	1	4	1	1	16	1	1
17.	0	0	0	0	0	1	0	0	0	0	1	0	0	1	0
18.	0	0	0	0	0	0	0	0	0	0	0	0	0	0	0
	9	6	9	8	5	8	10	8	9	41	22	27	187	46	69

$\Sigma Gj_I = 41$ $\Sigma Gj_{II} = 22$ $\Sigma Gj_{III} = 27$

$$Q_I = (5\text{-}1)\ \frac{(5\ [9^2+6^2+9^2+8^2+9^2]\ \text{-}41^2)}{5(41)\text{-}187} = 7.55$$

$$Q_{II} = (3\text{-}1)\ \frac{(3\ [5^2+8^2+9^2]\ \text{-}22^2)}{3(22)\text{-}46} = 2.60$$

$$Q_{III} = (3\text{-}1)\ \frac{(3\ [10^2+8^2+9^2]\ \text{-}27^2)}{3(27)\text{-}69} = 1.00$$

H_o = no significant difference between lower, middle, and upper subgroups' fixed sorts and their analyzed free sorts

df_I = 5-1) = 4	df_{II} = 3-1 = 2	df_{III} = 3-1 = 2
$p(\chi^2 \geqslant 9.49) = .05$	$p(\chi^2 \geqslant 5.99) = .05$	$p(\chi^2 \geqslant 5.99) = .05$
$7.55 < 9.49$	$2.60 < 5.99$	$1.00 < 5.99$

Therefore, H_o can *not* be rejected.

Figure 24
Cochran's Q Test for Significant Difference between Lower (Class I), Middle (Class II), and Upper (Class III), Subgroups' Fixed Sorts and Their Analyzed Free Sorts (as shown by the diameter diagram) for "Persons between Whom There is Mutual Social Exchange"

Card Number	Fixed Sorts I				Fixed Sorts II		Fixed Sorts III		Free Sorts	L_i I	L_i II	L_i III	L_i^2 I	L_i^2 II	L_i^2 III
1.	1	1	1	1	1	1	1	1	1	5	3	3	25	9	9
2.	0	0	0	0	0	0	0	0	0	0	0	0	0	0	0
3.	0	0	0	0	0	0	0	0	0	0	0	0	0	0	0
4.	1	0	1	1	1	0	0	1	1	4	2	2	16	4	4
5.	0	0	0	0	0	0	1	0	0	0	0	1	0	0	1
6.	0	1	1	1	1	1	1	0	1	4	3	2	16	9	4
7.	0	0	0	0	0	0	1	0	0	0	0	1	0	0	1
8.	0	0	0	0	0	0	1	0	0	0	0	1	0	0	1
9.	0	0	0	0	0	0	0	0	0	0	0	0	0	0	0
10.	0	0	0	0	0	0	0	1	0	0	0	1	0	0	1
11.	0	0	0	0	0	0	0	0	0	0	0	0	0	0	0
12.	0	0	0	0	0	0	0	0	0	0	0	0	0	0	0
13.	0	0	0	0	0	0	0	0	0	0	0	0	0	0	0
14.	0	0	0	0	0	0	0	1	0	0	0	1	0	0	1
15.	0	0	0	0	0	0	1	0	0	0	0	1	0	0	1
16.	0	0	0	0	0	0	0	0	0	0	0	0	0	0	0
17.	1	1	1	1	1	1	1	1	1	5	3	3	25	9	9
18.	0	1	1	0	0	0	0	1	0	2	0	1	4	0	1
	3	4	5	4	4	3	7	6	4	20	11	17	86	31	33

$\Sigma\, Gj_{I} = 20$ $\qquad$ $\Sigma\, Gj_{II} = 11$ $\qquad$ $\Sigma\, Gj_{III} = 17$

$$Q_{I} = (5\text{-}1)\ \frac{(5\,[3^2+4^2+5^2+4^2+4^2]\ \text{-}20^2)}{5(20)\text{-}86} = 2.86$$

$$Q_{II} = (3\text{-}1)\ \frac{(3\,[4^2+3^2+4^2]\ \text{-}11^2)}{3(11)\text{-}31} = 2.00$$

$$Q_{III} = (3\text{-}1)\ \frac{(3\,[7^2+6^2+4^2]\ \text{-}17^2)}{3(17)\text{-}33} = 1.56$$

H_o = no significant difference between lower, middle, and upper subgroups' fixed sorts and their analyzed free sorts

$df_I = 5\text{-}1 = 4$	$df_{II} = 3\text{-}1 = 2$	$df_{III} = 3\text{-}1 = 2$
$p(\chi^2 \geqslant 9.49) = .05$	$p(\chi^2 \geqslant 5.99) = .05$	$p(\chi^2 \geqslant 5.99) = .05$
$2.86 < 9.49$	$2.00 < 5.99$	$1.56 < 5.99$

Therefore, H_o can *not* be rejected.

Figure 25
Cochran's Q Test for Significant Difference between Lower (Class I), Middle (Class II), and Upper (Class III) Subgroups' Fixed Sorts and Their Analyzed Free Sorts (as shown by the diameter diagram) for "Higher Statuses" among "Persons between Whom There is Economic Exchange"

Card Number	Fixed Sorts I				Fixed Sorts II		Fixed Sorts III		Free Sorts	L_i I	L_i II	L_i III	L_i^2 I	L_i^2 II	L_i^2 III
1.	0	0	0	0	0	0	0	0	0	0	0	0	0	0	0
2.	0	0	0	0	0	1	0	0	0	0	1	0	0	1	0
3.	0	0	0	0	0	0	0	0	0	0	0	0	0	0	0
4.	0	1	0	0	0	0	0	0	0	1	0	0	1	0	0
5.	0	0	0	0	0	0	0	0	0	0	0	0	0	0	0
6.	0	0	0	0	0	0	0	0	0	0	0	0	0	0	0
7.	0	0	0	1	0	1	0	0	0	1	1	0	1	1	0
8.	0	0	0	0	0	0	0	0	0	0	0	0	0	0	0
9.	0	0	0	0	0	0	0	0	0	0	0	0	0	0	0
10.	1	1	0	0	1	0	0	0	1	3	2	1	9	4	1
11.	0	0	0	0	0	0	0	0	0	0	0	0	0	0	0
12.	0	0	0	0	0	0	0	0	0	0	0	0	0	0	0
13.	0	0	0	0	0	0	0	0	0	0	0	0	0	0	0
14.	0	0	0	0	1	0	0	0	0	0	1	0	0	1	0
15.	0	0	0	0	0	0	0	0	0	0	0	0	0	0	0
16.	0	1	0	0	0	0	0	0	0	1	0	0	1	0	0
17.	0	0	0	0	0	0	0	0	0	0	0	0	0	0	0
18.	0	0	0	1	0	0	0	0	0	1	0	0	1	0	0
	1	3	0	2	2	2	0	0	1	7	5	1	13	7	1

$\Sigma Gj_{I} = 7$ $\Sigma Gj_{II} = 5$ $\Sigma Gj_{III} = 1$

$$Q_{I} = (5\text{-}1)\ \frac{(5\ [1^2+3^2+0^2+2^2+1^2]\ \text{-}7^2)}{5(7)\text{-}13} = 4.73$$

$$Q_{II} = (3\text{-}1)\ \frac{(3\ [2^2+2^2+1^2]\ \text{-}5^2)}{3(5)\text{-}7} = 0.50$$

$$Q_{III} = (3\text{-}1)\ \frac{(3\ [0^2+0^2+1^2]\ \text{-}1^2)}{3(1)\text{-}1} = 2.00$$

H_o = no significant difference between lower, middle, and upper subgroups' fixed sorts and free sorts

$df_{I} = 5\text{-}1 = 4$	$df_{II} = 3\text{-}1 = 2$	$df_{III} = 3\text{-}1 = 2$
$p(\chi^2 \geqslant 9.49) = .05$	$p(\chi^2 \geqslant 5.99) = .05$	$p(\chi^2 \geqslant 5.99) = .05$
$4.73 < 9.49$	$0.50 < 5.99$	$2.00 < 5.99$

Therefore, H_o can *not* be rejected.

Figure 26

Cochran's Q Test for Significant Difference between Lower (Class I), Middle (Class II), and Upper (Class III) Subgroups' Fixed Sorts and Their Analyzed Free Sorts (as shown by the diameter diagram) for "Lower Statuses" among "Persons between Whom There is Economic Exchange"

Card Number	Fixed Sorts I				Fixed Sorts II		Fixed Sorts III		Free Sorts	L_i I	L_i II	L_i III	L_i^2 I	L_i^2 II	L_i^2 III
1.	0	0	0	0	0	0	0	0	0	0	0	0	0	0	0
2.	1	1	0	1	1	0	0	0	1	4	2	1	16	4	1
3.	1	1	0	1	1	1	1	0	1	4	3	2	16	9	4
4.	0	0	0	0	0	0	0	0	0	0	0	0	0	0	0
5.	0	0	0	0	0	0	0	0	0	0	0	0	0	0	0
6.	0	0	0	0	0	0	0	0	0	0	0	0	0	0	0
7.	0	0	0	0	0	0	0	0	0	0	0	0	0	0	0
8.	0	0	0	0	0	0	0	0	0	0	0	0	0	0	0
9.	0	0	0	0	0	0	1	0	0	0	0	1	0	0	1
10.	0	0	0	1	0	0	0	0	0	1	0	0	1	0	0
11.	0	0	0	0	0	0	0	0	0	0	0	0	0	0	0
12.	0	0	0	0	0	0	1	0	0	0	0	1	0	0	1
13.	0	0	0	0	0	0	1	0	0	0	0	1	0	0	1
14.	0	0	0	1	0	0	0	0	0	1	0	0	1	0	0
15.	0	0	0	0	0	0	1	0	0	0	0	1	0	0	1
16.	0	0	0	0	0	0	1	0	0	0	0	1	0	0	1
17.	0	0	0	0	0	0	0	0	0	0	0	0	0	0	0
18.	0	0	0	0	0	0	0	0	0	0	0	0	0	0	0
	2	2	0	4	2	1	6	0	2	10	5	8	34	13	10

$\Sigma\, Gj_{I} = 10$ $\Sigma\, Gj_{II} = 5$ $\Sigma\, Gj_{III} = 8$

$$Q_{I} = (5\text{-}1)\ \frac{(5\,[2^2+2^2+0^2+4^2+2^2]\ -10^2)}{5(10)-34} = 10.00$$

$$Q_{II} = (3\text{-}1)\ \frac{(3\,[2^2+1^2+2^2]\ -5^2)}{3(5)-13} = 2.00$$

$$Q_{III} = (3\text{-}1)\ \frac{(3\,[6^2+0^2+2^2]\ -8^2)}{3(8)-10} = 8.00$$

H_o = no significant difference between lower, middle, and upper subgroups' fixed sorts and their analyzed free sorts

$df_{I} = 5\text{-}1 = 4$	$df_{II} = 3\text{-}1 = 2$	$df_{III} = 3\text{-}1 = 2$
$p(\chi^2 \geqslant 9.49) = .05$	$p(\chi^2 \geqslant 5.99) = .05$	$p(\chi^2 \geqslant 5.99) = .05$
$10.00 > 9.49$	$2.00 < 5.99$	$8.00 > 5.99$

Therefore, H_o *can* be rejected for lower and upper subgroups but *not* for the middle one.

Figure 27

Cochran's Q Test for Significant Difference between Lower (Class I), Middle (Class II), and Upper (Class III) Subgroups' Fixed Sorts and Their Analyzed Free Sorts (as shown by the diameter diagram) for "Higher Statuses" among "Persons between Whom There is Political Exchange"

Card Number	Fixed Sorts I				Fixed Sorts II		Fixed Sorts III		Free Sorts	L_i I	L_i II	L_i III	L_i^2 I	L_i^2 II	L_i^2 III
1.	0	0	0	0	0	0	0	0	0	0	0	0	0	0	0
2.	0	0	0	0	0	0	0	0	0	0	0	0	0	0	0
3.	0	0	0	0	0	0	0	0	0	0	0	0	0	0	0
4.	0	0	0	0	0	0	0	0	0	0	0	0	0	0	0
5.	1	1	1	1	1	1	1	1	1	5	3	3	25	9	9
6.	0	0	0	0	0	0	0	0	0	0	0	0	0	0	0
7.	1	0	0	0	0	1	0	1	1	2	2	2	4	4	4
8.	1	1	1	1	1	1	1	1	1	5	3	3	25	9	9
9.	0	0	1	0	1	0	0	0	0	1	1	0	1	1	0
10.	0	0	0	0	0	0	0	0	0	0	0	0	0	0	0
11.	0	1	1	0	0	1	0	0	0	2	1	0	4	1	0
12	0	0	0	0	0	0	0	0	0	0	0	0	0	0	0
13.	0	0	0	0	0	0	0	0	0	0	0	0	0	0	0
14.	0	0	0	0	0	0	0	0	0	0	0	0	0	0	0
15.	0	0	0	0	0	0	0	0	0	0	0	0	0	0	0
16.	1	0	1	1	0	0	0	0	1	4	1	1	16	1	1
17.	0	0	0	0	0	0	0	0	0	0	0	0	0	0	0
18.	0	0	0	0	0	0	0	0	0	0	0	0	0	0	0
	4	3	5	3	3	4	2	3	4	19	11	9	75	25	23

$\Sigma Gj_{I} = 19$ $\Sigma Gj_{II} = 11$ $\Sigma Gj_{III} = 9$

$$Q_{I} = (5\text{-}1)\ \frac{(5\ [4^2+3^2+5^2+3^2+4^2]\ -19^2)}{5(19)\text{-}75} = 2.80$$

$$Q_{II} = (3\text{-}1)\ \frac{(3\ [3^2+4^2+4^2]\ -\ 11^2)}{3(11)\text{-}25} = 0.50$$

$$Q_{III} = (3\text{-}1)\ \frac{(3\ [2^2+3^2+4^2]\ -9^2)}{3(9)\text{-}23} = 3.00$$

H_o = no significant difference between lower, middle, and upper subgroups' fixed sorts and their analyzed free sorts

$df_{I} = 5\text{-}1 = 4$	$df_{II} = 3\text{-}1 = 2$	$df_{III} = 3\text{-}1 = 2$
$p(\chi^2 \geqslant 9.49) = .05$	$p(\chi^2 \geqslant 5.99) = .05$	$p(\chi^2 \geqslant 5.99) = .05$
$2.80 < 9.49$	$0.50 < 5.99$	$3.00 < 5.99$

Therefore, H_o can *not* be rejected.

Figure 28

Cochran's Q Test for Significant Difference between Lower (Class I), Middle (Class II), and Upper (Class III) Subgroups' Fixed Sorts and Their Analyzed Free Sorts (as shown by the diameter diagram) for "Lower Statuses" among "Persons between Whom There is Political Exchange"

Card Number	Fixed Sorts								Free Sorts	L_i			L_i^2		
	I				II		III			I	II	III	I	II	III
1.	0	0	0	0	0	1	0	0	0	0	1	0	0	1	0
2.	0	0	0	0	0	0	0	0	0	0	0	0	0	0	0
3.	0	0	0	0	0	0	0	0	0	0	0	0	0	0	0
4.	0	0	0	0	0	1	0	0	0	0	1	0	0	1	0
5.	0	0	0	0	0	0	0	0	0	0	0	0	0	0	0
6.	0	0	0	0	0	0	0	0	0	0	0	0	0	0	0
7.	0	1	1	0	0	0	0	0	0	2	0	0	4	0	0
8.	0	0	0	0	0	0	0	0	0	0	0	0	0	0	0
9.	1	1	0	1	0	0	1	0	1	4	1	2	16	1	4
10.	0	0	0	0	0	0	0	0	0	0	0	0	0	0	0
11.	1	0	0	1	0	0	1	0	1	3	1	2	9	1	4
12.	1	0	1	1	1	0	1	1	1	4	2	3	16	4	9
13.	1	0	1	1	0	1	1	1	1	4	2	3	16	4	9
14.	0	0	0	0	0	0	0	0	0	0	0	0	0	0	0
15.	1	1	1	1	1	0	1	1	1	5	2	3	25	4	9
16.	0	0	0	0	0	0	0	0	0	0	0	0	0	0	0
17.	0	0	0	0	0	1	0	0	0	0	1	0	0	1	0
18.	0	0	0	0	0	0	0	0	0	0	0	0	0	0	0
	5	3	4	5	2	4	5	3	5	22	11	13	86	17	35

$\Sigma Gj_{I} = 22$ $\qquad$ $\Sigma Gj_{II} = 11$ $\qquad$ $\Sigma Gj_{III} = 13$

$$Q_{I} = (5\text{-}1)\ \frac{(5\ [5^2+3^2+4^2+5^2+5^2]\ -22^2)}{5(22)\text{-}86} = 2.67$$

$$Q_{II} = (3\text{-}1)\ \frac{(3\ [2^2+4^2+5^2]\ -11^2)}{3(11)\text{-}17} = 1.75$$

$$Q_{III} = (3\text{-}1)\ \frac{(3\ [5^2+3^2+5^2]\ -13^2)}{3(13)\text{-}35} = 0.53$$

H_o = no significant difference between lower, middle, and upper subgroups' fixed sorts and their analyzed free sorts

$df_{I} = 5\text{-}1 = 4$	$df_{II} = 3\text{-}1 = 2$	$df_{III} = 3\text{-}1 = 2$
$p(\chi^2 \geqslant 9.49) = .05$	$p(\chi^2 \geqslant 5.99) = .05$	$p(\chi^2 \geqslant 5.99) = .05$
$2.67 < 9.49$	$1.75 < 5.99$	$0.53 < 5.99$

Therefore, H_o can *not* be rejected.

Figure 29
Cochran's Q. Test for Significant Difference between Younger (35-36), Middle-Aged (45-51), and Older (60-80) Subgroups' Fixed Sorts and Their Analyzed Free Sorts (as shown by the diameter diagram) for "Persons between Whom There is Economic Exchange"

Card	Fixed Sorts								Free	L_i			L_i^2		
Number	Younger		Middle			Older			Sorts	Y	M	O	Y	M	O
1.	0	0	0	0	0	0	0	0	0	0	0	0	0	0	0
2.	1	1	1	1	1	1	1	1	1	3	4	4	9	16	16
3.	1	1	1	1	1	1	1	1	1	3	4	4	9	16	16
4.	0	0	0	0	1	0	0	0	0	0	1	0	0	1	0
5.	1	0	0	0	0	0	0	0	0	1	0	0	1	0	0
6.	0	0	0	0	0	0	0	1	0	0	0	1	0	0	1
7.	0	0	1	0	0	0	0	1	0	0	1	1	0	1	1
8.	1	0	0	0	0	0	0	0	0	1	0	0	1	0	0
9.	1	1	0	1	0	0	0	0	0	2	1	0	4	1	0
10.	1	1	1	0	1	1	1	0	1	3	3	3	9	9	9
11.	1	0	0	0	0	0	0	0	0	1	0	0	1	0	0
12.	0	1	0	0	0	1	0	0	0	1	0	1	1	0	1
13.	1	1	0	0	0	0	0	0	0	2	0	0	4	0	0
14.	1	1	1	0	0	0	1	1	0	2	1	2	4	1	4
15.	1	1	0	0	0	0	0	0	0	2	0	0	4	0	0
16.	1	1	0	0	1	0	0	1	0	2	1	1	4	1	1
17.	0	0	0	0	0	0	0	0	0	0	0	0	0	0	0
18.	0	1	1	0	0	0	0	1	0	1	1	1	1	1	1
	11	10	6	3	5	4	4	7	3	24	17	18	52	47	50

$\Sigma Gj_Y = 24$ $\Sigma Gj_M = 17$ $\Sigma Gj_O = 18$

$$Q_Y = (3\text{-}1) \frac{(3 [11^2+10^2+3^2] -24^2)}{3(24)\text{-}52} = 11.40$$

$$Q_M = (4\text{-}1) \frac{(4 [6^2+3^2+5^2+3^2] -17^2)}{4(17)\text{-}47} = 3.86$$

$$Q_O = (4\text{-}1) \frac{(4 [4^2+4^2+7^2+3^2] -18^2)}{4(18)\text{-}50} = 4.91$$

H_O = no significant difference between younger, middle-aged, and older subgroups' fixed sorts and their analyzed free sorts

$df_Y = 3\text{-}1 = 2$	$df_M = 4\text{-}1 = 3$	$df_O = 4\text{-}1 = 3$
$p(\chi^2 \geqslant 5.99) = .05$	$p(\chi^2 \geqslant 7.82) = .05$	$p(\chi^2 \geqslant 7.82) = .05$
$11.40 > 5.99$	$3.86 < 7.82$	$4.91 < 7.82$

Therefore, H_O *can* be rejected for the younger subgroup, but *not* for the middle-aged or older subgroups.

Figure 30
Cochran's Q Test for Significant Difference between Younger (35-36), Middle-Aged (45-51), and Older (60-80) Subgroups' Fixed Sorts and Their Analyzed Free Sorts (as shown by the diameter diagram) for "Persons between Whom There is Political Exchange"

Card Number	Younger		Fixed Sorts Middle			Older			Free Sorts	L_i Y	L_i M	L_i O	L_i^2 Y	L_i^2 M	L_i^2 O
1.	0	0	0	0	0	0	1	0	0	0	0	1	0	0	1
2.	0	1	0	0	0	0	0	0	0	1	0	0	1	0	0
3.	1	1	0	0	0	0	0	0	0	2	0	0	4	0	0
4.	0	0	0	0	0	0	1	0	0	0	0	1	0	0	1
5.	1	1	1	1	1	1	1	1	1	3	4	4	9	16	16
6.	0	0	0	0	0	0	0	0	0	0	0	0	0	0	0
7.	1	0	0	1	1	1	1	0	1	2	3	3	4	9	9
8.	1	1	1	1	1	1	1	1	1	3	4	4	9	16	16
9.	0	1	1	1	1	1	0	1	1	2	4	3	4	16	9
10.	0	1	0	0	0	0	0	0	0	1	0	0	1	0	0
11.	1	1	1	1	1	1	1	0	1	3	4	3	9	16	9
12.	1	1	1	1	0	1	0	1	1	3	3	3	9	9	9
13.	1	1	1	1	0	1	1	0	1	3	3	3	9	9	9
14.	0	0	0	0	0	0	0	0	0	0	0	0	0	0	0
15.	1	1	1	1	1	1	0	1	1	3	4	3	9	16	9
16.	0	0	1	1	0	1	0	0	1	1	3	2	1	9	4
17.	0	0	0	0	0	0	1	0	0	0	0	1	0	0	1
18.	0	0	0	0	0	0	0	0	0	0	0	0	0	0	0
	8	10	8	9	6	9	8	5	9	27	32	31	69	116	93

$\Sigma Gj_Y = 27$ $\Sigma Gj_M = 32$ $\Sigma Gj_O = 31$

$$Q_Y = (3\text{-}1)\frac{(3\,[8^2+10^2+9^2]-27^2)}{3(27)-69} = 0.67$$

$$Q_M = (4\text{-}1)\frac{(4\,[8^2+9^2+6^2+9^2]-32^2)}{4(32)-116} = 6.00$$

$$Q_O = (4\text{-}1)\frac{(4\,[9^2+8^2+5^2+9^2]-31^2)}{4(31)-93} = 4.16$$

H_O = no significant difference between younger, middle-aged, and older subgroups' fixed sorts and their analyzed free sorts

$df_Y = 3\text{-}1 = 2$
$p(\chi^2 \geqslant 5.99) = .05$
$0.67 < 5.99$

$df_M = 4\text{-}1 = 3$
$p(\chi^2 \geqslant 7.82) = .05$
$6.00 < 7.82$

$df_O = 4\text{-}1 = 3$
$p(\chi^2 \geqslant 7.82) = .05$
$4.16 < 7.82$

Therefore, H_O can *not* be rejected.

Figure 31
Cochran's Q. Test for Significant Difference between Younger (35-36), Middle-Aged (45-51), and Older (60-80) Subgroups' Fixed Sorts and Their Analyzed Free Sorts (as shown by the diameter diagram) for "Persons between Whom There is Mutual Social Exchange"

Card Number	Fixed Sorts Younger		Fixed Sorts Middle			Fixed Sorts Older			Free Sorts	L_i Y	L_i M	L_i O	L_i^2 Y	L_i^2 M	L_i^2 O
1.	1	1	1	1	1	1	1	1	1	3	4	4	9	16	16
2.	0	0	0	0	0	0	0	0	0	0	0	0	0	0	0
3.	0	0	0	0	0	0	0	0	0	0	0	0	0	0	0
4.	1	0	1	1	0	1	0	1	1	2	3	3	4	9	9
5.	0	1	0	0	0	0	0	0	0	1	0	0	1	0	0
6.	0	1	1	0	1	1	1	1	1	2	3	4	4	9	16
7.	0	1	0	0	0	0	0	0	0	1	0	0	1	0	0
8.	0	1	0	0	0	0	0	0	0	1	0	0	1	0	0
9.	0	0	0	0	0	0	0	0	0	0	0	0	0	0	0
10.	0	0	0	0	0	0	0	0	0	0	0	0	0	0	0
11.	1	0	0	0	0	0	0	0	0	1	0	0	1	0	0
12.	0	0	0	0	0	0	0	0	0	0	0	0	0	0	0
13.	0	0	0	0	0	0	0	0	0	0	0	0	0	0	0
14.	1	0	0	0	0	0	0	0	0	1	0	0	1	0	0
15.	0	1	0	0	0	0	0	0	0	1	0	0	1	0	0
16.	0	0	0	0	0	0	0	0	0	0	0	0	0	0	0
17.	1	1	1	1	1	1	1	1	1	3	4	4	9	16	16
18.	1	0	0	0	1	1	0	0	0	1	1	1	1	1	1
	6	7	4	3	4	5	3	4	4	17	15	16	33	51	58

$\Sigma Gj_Y = 17$ $\qquad \Sigma Gj_M = 15$ $\qquad \Sigma Gj_O = 16$

$$Q_Y = (3\text{-}1) \frac{(3\,[6^2+7^2+4^2]\,-17^2)}{3(17)\text{-}33} = 1.56$$

$$Q_M = (4\text{-}1) \frac{(4\,[4^2+3^2+4^2+4^2]\,-15^2)}{4(15)\text{-}51} = 1.00$$

$$Q_O = (4\text{-}1) \frac{(4\,[5^2+3^2+4^2+4^2]\,-16^2)}{4(16)\text{-}58} = 4.00$$

H_o = no significant difference between younger, middle-aged, and older subgroups' fixed sorts and their analyzed free sorts

$df_Y = 3\text{-}1 = 2$
$p(\chi^2 \geqslant 5.99) = .05$
$1.56 < 5.99$

$df_M = 4\text{-}1 = 3$
$p(\chi^2 \geqslant 7.82) = .05$
$1.00 < 7.82$

$df_O = 4\text{-}1 = 3$
$p(\chi^2 \geqslant 7.82) = .05$
$4.00 < 7.82$

Therefore, H_o can *not* be rejected.

Figure 32
Cochran's Q Test for Significant Difference between Younger (35-36), Middle-Aged (45-51), and Older (60-80) Subgroups' Fixed Sorts and Their Analyzed Free Sorts (as shown by the diameter diagram) for "Higher Statuses" among "Persons between Whom There is Economic Exchange"

Card Number	Fixed Sorts Younger		Fixed Sorts Middle			Fixed Sorts Older			Free Sorts	L_i Y	L_i M	L_i O	L_i^2 Y	L_i^2 M	L_i^2 O
1.	0	0	0	0	0	0	0	0	0	0	0	0	0	0	0
2.	0	0	0	0	0	0	1	0	0	0	0	1	0	0	1
3.	0	0	0	0	0	0	0	0	0	0	0	0	0	0	0
4.	0	0	0	0	1	0	0	0	0	0	1	0	0	1	0
5.	0	0	0	0	0	0	0	0	0	0	0	0	0	0	0
6.	0	0	0	0	0	0	0	0	0	0	0	0	0	0	0
7.	0	0	1	0	0	0	1	0	0	0	1	1	0	1	1
8.	0	0	0	0	0	0	0	0	0	0	0	0	0	0	0
9.	0	0	0	0	0	0	0	0	0	0	0	0	0	0	0
10.	0	0	0	1	1	0	0	1	1	0	3	2	0	9	4
11.	0	0	0	0	0	0	0	0	0	0	0	0	0	0	0
12.	0	0	0	0	0	0	0	0	0	0	0	0	0	0	0
13.	0	0	0	0	0	0	0	0	0	0	0	0	0	0	0
14.	0	0	0	0	0	0	0	1	0	0	0	1	0	0	1
15.	0	0	0	0	0	0	0	0	0	0	0	0	0	0	0
16.	0	0	0	0	1	0	0	0	0	0	1	0	0	1	0
17.	0	0	0	0	0	0	0	0	0	0	0	0	0	0	0
18.	0	0	1	0	0	0	0	0	0	0	1	0	0	1	0
	0	0	2	1	3	0	2	2	1	1	7	5	1	13	7

$\Sigma\, Gj_Y = 1$ $\Sigma\, Gj_M = 7$ $\Sigma\, Gj_O = 5$

$$Q_Y = (3\text{-}1)\ \frac{(3\,[0^2+0^2+1^2]\ -1^2)}{3(1)\text{-}1} = 2.00$$

$$Q_M = (4\text{-}1)\ \frac{(4\,[2^2+1^2+3^2+1^2]\ -7^2)}{4(7)\text{-}13} = 2.20$$

$$Q_O = (4\text{-}1)\ \frac{(4\,[0^2+2^2+2^2+1^2]\ -5^2)}{4(5)\text{-}7} = 2.54$$

H_o = no significant difference between younger, middle-aged, and older subgroups' fixed sorts and their analyzed free sorts

$df_Y = 3\text{-}1 = 2$	$df_M = 4\text{-}1 = 3$	$df_O = 4\text{-}1 = 3$
$p(\chi^2 \geqslant 5.99) = .05$	$p(\chi^2 \geqslant 7.82) = .05$	$p(\chi^2 \geqslant 7.82) = .05$
$2.00 < 5.99$	$2.20 < 7.82$	$2.54 < 7.82$

Therefore, H_o can *not* be rejected.

Figure 33
Cochran's Q Test for Significant Difference between Younger (35-36), Middle-Aged (45-51), and Older (60-80) Subgroups' Fixed Sorts and Their Analyzed Free Sorts (as shown by the diameter diagram) for "Lower Statuses" among "Persons between Whom There is Economic Exchange"

Card	Fixed Sorts								Free		L_i			L_i^2	
Number	Younger		Middle			Older			Sorts	Y	M	O	Y	M	O
1.	0	0	0	0	0	0	0	0	0	0	0	0	0	0	0
2.	0	0	1	1	1	0	0	1	1	1	4	2	1	16	4
3.	0	1	1	1	1	0	1	1	1	2	4	3	4	16	9
4.	0	0	0	0	0	0	0	0	0	0	0	0	0	0	0
5.	0	0	0	0	0	0	0	0	0	0	0	0	0	0	0
6.	0	0	0	0	0	0	0	0	0	0	0	0	0	0	0
7.	0	0	0	0	0	0	0	0	0	0	0	0	0	0	0
8.	0	0	0	0	0	0	0	0	0	0	0	0	0	0	0
9.	0	1	0	0	0	0	0	0	0	1	0	0	1	0	0
10.	0	0	1	0	0	0	0	0	0	0	1	0	0	1	0
11.	0	0	0	0	0	0	0	0	0	0	0	0	0	0	0
12.	0	1	0	0	0	0	0	0	0	1	0	0	1	0	0
13.	0	1	0	0	0	0	0	0	0	1	0	0	1	0	0
14.	0	0	1	0	0	0	0	0	0	0	1	0	0	1	0
15.	0	1	0	0	0	0	0	0	0	1	0	0	1	0	0
16.	0	1	0	0	0	0	0	0	0	1	0	0	1	0	0
17.	0	0	0	0	0	0	0	0	0	0	0	0	0	0	0
18.	0	0	0	0	0	0	0	0	0	0	0	0	0	0	0
	0	6	4	2	2	0	1	2	2	8	10	5	10	34	13

$\Sigma Gj_Y = 8$ $\Sigma Gj_M = 10$ $\Sigma Gj_O = 5$

$$Q_Y = (3\text{-}1) \frac{(3\,[0^2+6^2+3^3]\,-8^2)}{3(8)\text{-}10} = 8.00$$

$$Q_M = (4\text{-}1) \frac{(4\,[4^2+2^2+2^2+2^2]\,-10^2)}{4(10)\text{-}34} = 6.00$$

$$Q_O = (4\text{-}1) \frac{(4\,[0^2+1^2+2^2+2^2]\,-5^2)}{4(5)\text{-}13} = 4.71$$

H_o = no significant difference between younger, middle-aged, and older subgroups' fixed sorts and their analyzed free sorts

$df_Y = 3\text{-}1 = 2$	$df_M = 4\text{-}1 = 3$	$df_O = 4\text{-}1 = 3$
$p(\chi^2 \geqslant 5.99) = .05$	$p(\chi^2 \geqslant 7.82) = .05$	$p(\chi^2 \geqslant 7.82) = .05$
$8.00 > 5.99$	$6.00 < 7.82$	$4.71 < 7.82$

Therefore, H_o *can* be rejected for the younger subgroup but *not* for the middle-aged or older ones.

Figure 34
Cochran's Q Test for Significant Difference between Younger (35-36), Middle-Aged (45-51), and Older (60-80) Subgroups' Fixed Sorts and Their Analyzed Free Sorts (as shown by the diameter diagram) for "Higher Statuses" among "Persons between Whom There is Political Exchange"

Card Number	Fixed Sorts Younger		Fixed Sorts Middle			Fixed Sorts Older			Free Sorts	L_i Y	L_i M	L_i O	L_i^2 Y	L_i^2 M	L_i^2 O
1.	0	0	0	0	0	0	0	0	0	0	0	0	0	0	0
2.	0	0	0	0	0	0	0	0	0	0	0	0	0	0	0
3.	0	0	0	0	0	0	0	0	0	0	0	0	0	0	0
4.	0	0	0	0	0	0	0	0	0	0	0	0	0	0	0
5.	1	1	1	1	1	1	1	1	1	3	4	4	9	16	16
6.	0	0	0	0	0	0	0	0	0	0	0	0	0	0	0
7.	1	0	0	1	0	0	1	0	1	2	2	2	4	4	4
8.	1	1	1	1	1	1	1	1	1	3	4	4	9	16	16
9.	0	0	0	0	0	1	0	1	0	0	0	2	0	0	4
10.	0	0	0	0	0	0	0	0	0	0	0	0	0	0	0
11.	0	0	0	0	1	1	1	0	0	0	1	2	0	1	4
12.	0	0	0	0	0	0	0	0	0	0	0	0	0	0	0
13.	0	0	0	0	0	0	0	0	0	0	0	0	0	0	0
14.	0	0	0	0	0	0	0	0	0	0	0	0	0	0	0
15.	0	0	0	0	0	0	0	0	0	0	0	0	0	0	0
16.	0	0	1	1	0	1	1	0	1	0	3	2	0	9	4
17.	0	0	0	0	0	0	0	0	0	0	0	0	0	0	0
18.	0	0	0	0	0	0	0	0	0	0	0	0	0	0	0
	3	2	3	4	3	5	4	3	4	9	14	16	23	46	48

$\Sigma Gj_Y = 9$ $\Sigma Gj_M = 14$ $\Sigma Gj_O = 16$

$$Q_Y = (3\text{-}1)\frac{(3\,[3^2+2^2+4^2]\,-9^2)}{3(9)-23} = 3.00$$

$$Q_M = (4\text{-}1)\frac{(4\,[3^2+4^2+3^2+4^2]\,-14^2)}{4(14)-46} = 1.20$$

$$Q_O = (4\text{-}1)\frac{(4\,[5^2+4^2+3^2+4^2]\,-16^2)}{4(16)-48} = 1.50$$

H_o = no significant difference between younger, middle-aged, and older subgroups' fixed sorts and their analyzed free sorts

$df_Y = 3\text{-}1 = 2$	$df_M = 4\text{-}1 = 3$	$df_O = 4\text{-}1 = 3$
$p(\chi^2 \geqslant 5.99) - .05$	$p(\chi^2 \geqslant 7.82) = .05$	$p(\chi^2 \geqslant 7.82) = .05$
$3.00 < 5.99$	$1.20 < 7.82$	$1.50 < 7.82$

Therefore, H_o can *not* be rejected.

Figure 35
Cochran's Q Test for Significant Difference between Younger (35-36), Middle-Aged (45-51), and Older (60-80) Subgroups' Fixed Sorts and Their Analyzed Free Sorts (as shown by the diameter diagram) for "Lower Statuses" among "Persons between Whom There is Political Exchange"

Card Number	Fixed Sorts Younger		Fixed Sorts Middle			Fixed Sorts Older			Free Sorts	L_i Y	L_i M	L_i O	L_i^2 Y	L_i^2 M	L_i^2 O
1.	0	0	0	0	0	0	1	0	0	0	0	1	0	0	1
2.	0	0	0	0	0	0	0	0	0	0	0	0	0	0	0
3.	0	0	0	0	0	0	0	0	0	0	0	0	0	0	0
4.	0	0	0	0	0	0	1	0	0	0	0	1	0	0	1
5.	0	0	0	0	0	0	0	0	0	0	0	0	0	0	0
6.	0	0	0	0	0	0	0	0	0	0	0	0	0	0	0
7.	0	0	0	0	1	1	0	0	0	0	1	1	0	1	1
8.	0	0	0	0	0	0	0	0	0	0	0	0	0	0	0
9.	0	1	1	1	1	0	0	0	1	2	4	1	4	16	1
10.	0	0	0	0	0	0	0	0	0	0	0	0	0	0	0
11.	0	1	1	1	0	0	0	0	1	2	3	1	4	9	1
12.	1	1	1	1	0	1	0	1	1	3	3	3	9	9	9
13.	1	1	1	1	0	1	1	0	1	3	3	3	9	9	9
14.	0	0	0	0	0	0	0	0	0	0	0	0	0	0	0
15.	1	1	1	1	1	1	0	1	1	3	4	3	9	16	9
16.	0	0	0	0	0	0	0	0	0	0	0	0	0	0	0
17.	0	0	0	0	0	0	0	0	0	0	0	0	0	0	0
18.	0	0	0	0	0	0	0	0	0	0	0	0	0	0	0
	3	5	5	5	3	4	4	2	5	13	18	15	35	60	33

$\Sigma\, Gj_Y = 13$ $\Sigma\, Gj_M = 18$ $\Sigma\, Gj_O = 15$

$$Q_Y = (3\text{-}1)\,\frac{(3\,[3^2+5^2+5^2]\,-13^2)}{3(13)\text{-}35} = 4.00$$

$$Q_M = (4\text{-}1)\,\frac{(4\,[5^2+5^2+3^2+5^2]\,-18^2)}{4(18)\text{-}60} = 3.00$$

$$Q_O = (4\text{-}1)\,\frac{(4\,[4^2+4^2+2^2+5^2]\,-15^2)}{4(15)\text{-}33} = 2.11$$

H_o = no significant difference between younger, middle-aged, and older subgroups' fixed sorts and their analyzed free sorts

$df_Y = 3\text{-}1 = 2$	$df_M = 4\text{-}1 = 3$	$df_O = 4\text{-}1 = 3$
$p(\chi^2 \geqslant 5.99) = .05$	$p(\chi^2 \geqslant 7.82) = .05$	$p(\chi^2 \geqslant 7.82) = .05$
$4.00 < 5.99$	$3.00 < 7.82$	$2.11 < 7.82$

Therefore, H_o can *not* be rejected.

the only significant variation concerns "persons . . . economic exchange" and its "lower status" subcategory. Earlier, the cause for such variation was traced to the fixed sorts of the two younger, upper-class informants. Since one of these men was Druze, the other Christian, it is possible that their sorts alone cause the significant differences shown in Appendixes 2*a* and 2*f*. To investigate this possibility, one may drop their fixed sorts from consideration and examine what effect sectarian membership has for all other informants. When this is done, Appendix 2*b* shows that there is no significant difference for "persons . . . economic exchange." That is, the variation evident in Appendix 2*a* disappears when results for the two younger, upper-class men are removed. On the other hand, Appendix 2*g* gives a slightly different picture for the "lower status" subcategory. Dropping the results for the two younger, upper-class informants eliminates the significant difference between fixed and free sorts for the Christian subgroup but not for the Druze one. Druze results, however, are just barely significant: a change of one sort would have brought them within the .05 limit. Even for the "persons . . . economic exchange" and "lower status" categories, then, there is very little support for the association of sorting differences with sectarian subgroups, once the effects of class and age are accounted for. Accordingly, it seems reasonable to conclude that significant differences in sorting (and the conceptual structures implied by them) are not correlated with religious affiliation.

In terms of the dimension of political faction, the informant sample was composed of four Yazbakis and four Junblāṭṭis. The statistical analyses of sorts by these subgroups are given as Appendixes 3*a* through 3*h*. This time there is a significant difference between each faction's fixed sorts and the whole sample's free sorts only for the "persons . . . economic exchange" category (App. 3*a*). When the effects of class and age are accounted for—i.e., when the results for the two younger, upper-class informants are removed from consideration—the sorts belonging to the other members of both factions are not significantly different from the free sorts for this category, as Appendix 3*b* shows. Thus, it again is reasonable to conclude that membership in either faction is not correlated with significant differences in sorting.

For all four dimensions—class, age, sect, and faction—there are no significant differences between fixed and free sorts for "persons . . . political exchange" or "persons . . . mutual social exchange," nor for "higher" and "lower" statuses among the former. On the other hand, there *are* significant differences between fixed and free sorts for "persons . . . economic exchange" and sometimes for its "lower status" subcategory. These differences, in the main, are correlated with the socio-economic class and age of informants but not with their religious or factional affiliations. In a sense, then, assumptions underlying a major concept in what Hymes, Gumperz, and others (Gumperz and Hymes 1964) have called an "ethnography of communication" are given empirical reference and support. Differences in semantic structure have been related to differences in social structure: members of one class and age subgroup have been shown to conceive of "economic exchange statuses" in one way; members of other class and age subgroups, in a different way. However, before the more complex concepts in this approach–those like "elaborate versus restricted codes" (Bernstein 1964) or "norms of social appropriateness" (Gumperz 1964) or "verbal repertoire" (Hymes 1964)–become useful field tools, in my opinion, much more basic confirmation and clarification of underlying concepts needs to be done. In this way an interesting but as yet mainly programmatic theoretical approach can be given a more empirical foundation.

SUMMARY AND CONCLUSIONS

In the present section, results of a psycholinguistic experiment have been used to show both that and how the social exchange model of wāsiṭa has a kind of "psychological reality" for a sample of Barouki informants. First, the discussion turned on how and why a sample of eight informants was chosen to represent subgroups extant in the village population. Second, the manner of choosing terms for eighteen economic, political, and social statuses was covered. Third, the administration of the experiment was explained by indicating how terms were presented to informants and what kinds of sorting they were asked to make with those terms. And fourth, analyses were made of sorting results: free sorts were clustered into the hierarchical semantic structures concerned; then fixed-sort results were compared to these clusters. Such comparisons provide clues to what semantic contrasts were present in the free-sort results and show how different conceptions of semantic structure may be related to differences in social structure. In reference to the particular focus of this monograph, the term wasīṭ was shown to designate either a "medial, superior, political exchange status" or a "medial, mutual, social exchange status" for all informants, regardless of their class, age, sect, or faction. By implication, then, wāsiṭa is conceived to be what a wasīṭ offers in a given transaction. That is, it is a process used as a reward by a party in social exchange with an alter in order to generate either a power or a mutual relationship between them.

IV

CONCLUSION

The purpose of this study was to describe and analyze the process of wāsiṭa as it operates in a Lebanese village composed of subgroups organized in terms of different principles–sects, classes, factions, etc. In Section 1 the study began with a brief consideration of salient aspects of Lebanese geography and history, emphasizing those factors which have contributed to creating the country's abundant social diversity within a relatively small territory. Next, the discussion turned to how social scientists have attempted to deal with, or more often to avoid, this diversity. As an approach to a more integrated description of Lebanese society, the study advocated examining wāsiṭa as a process which operates on, and between, micro and macro levels of that society in economic, political, and social contexts. Then there followed a more detailed analysis of work done by anthropologists Victor Ayoub and Laura Nader on wāsiṭa as a conflict-regulation process. To expand their insights, and to avoid certain problems in their work, an amended version of Peter Blau's conceptions of social exchange was used as a framework for studying what wāsiṭa is and how it functions. As the discussion indicated, a key aspect of Blau's model is the attention it draws to participants' values and conceptions of the actors, rewards, and processes of social exchange.

In Section 2, this model was applied to data from the ethnographic context of the study. After locating the research site at Barouk, a village in south-central Mount Lebanon, the monograph explained why social interaction was, at first, limited to a small number of villagers. This limitation permitted concentration to be focused on visiting behavior, the major means of social interaction in the village. Several examples were used to indicate the various kinds and contexts of visits exchanged and how some of them lead to mutual relationships, others to power relationships, between the persons visiting and visited. The understanding of relationships based on power social exchange, in turn, provided a valuable insight into similarities and differences between social ties such as those which exist today between a political leader and his followers, or those which existed in the past between a feudal lord and his charges. For instance, both of these sets of relationships concern exchanges of "protection" for "support," but the former more frequently involves the use of wāsiṭa to tap services provided by outside sources of power (e.g., the government administration). As the discussion in Section 2 showed, mobilizing such relationships in support of the field research in Barouk was an important step in extending that research throughout the village. Utilizing the acceptance provided by such relationships, a large number of households broadly representative of all groups in the village was interviewed. The results of these interviews, in turn, provided an interesting picture of social stratification. This picture, when combined with case examples of interaction among villagers (and between them and outsiders) indicated that wāsiṭa is a process which can function as a reward traded in social exchange. If, during several transactions, one party returns goods and/or services culturally equivalent in value to the intermediary service provided by another party, then a relationship based on mutual social exchange is established between the parties. If, however, those goods and/or services are not considered to be culturally equivalent in value but transactions continue all the same, a relationship based on power social exchange ensues. Just such a relationship is discussed in Section 2 to show how a national-level political leader has been "capturing" followers from his traditional rivals through exchanges of his wāsiṭa for their political support.

Since the conceptions of persons involved in exchanges are such an important part of the social exchange model, Section 3 provided a detailed study of them. Describing how a sample of informants was chosen so as to represent all significant subgroups in the village, the discussion then considered how terms designating various statuses were selected for study. Following this was an account of the ways terms were presented to informants in a psycholinguistic experiment and what the results of that experiment were. The analyses of these results indicated that Baroukis, as a whole, conceive of wāsiṭa as a process which can be used as a reward in either "mutual social exchange" or "political exchange." Furthermore, those analyses indicated that there were significant differences in sorting among the different class and age subgroups constituting the informant sample in regard to economic exchange. Informants belonging both to the upper class and the younger subgroup tended to find economic senses of meaning for more terms than did informants of other class or age subgroups. Examining the results in terms of other kinds of subgroups, however, did not reveal significant differences in sorting, once the effects of class and age were accounted for. That is, substantially the same conceptions of economic exchange prevailed among the various sects and factions constituting the informant sample.

It seems fitting to close this monograph with a few comments on the kinds of future research which might emanate from it. As was mentioned during the discussion of the play put on by the Barouk youth club, diachronic study might be informative. One could return to Barouk after a given time period to learn which of the things described in this monograph have changed, which remained the same, and why.

Another focus for future research might be the links between kinship organization and factional alliances in a "plural" village like Barouk. As was discussed in Section 2, Arabic ʿayli is probably better glossed as "family" for the Barouk data. However, several smaller "families" in one of the two traditional factions were sometimes spoken of as jubūb ("clans") of the largest ʿayli of the same sect in their faction.[1] Each of these smaller "families" had a different last name, at least two of them were identified with their own section of the village, and one of them had a separate association to promote the common interests of its members. This situation was viewed with some humor by members of the other faction, who claimed their opponents were not really unified but only "wrapped around each other" (Ar. *biliffū ʿala baʿdhom*). This use of a form of the verb *laffa* (Eng. "to wrap up, envelop") may provide an important clue to elucidating the links between alliances and kinship. For example, Antoun (1972:88) reports that an informant in the Jordanian village of Kafr al-Ma made a very similar distinction: he claimed that his clan was stronger than other local ones because "there is no wrapping around it" (Ar. *mā fīha lafāf*). Still further afield, Peters (1970*b*:383-84) says that the Bedouin of Cyrenaica use the term *laff* to refer to "grafts," i.e., persons residing with, and allied to, a section of "free" tribesmen without becoming part of their genealogical charter. Finally, the anthropological literature on Berber societies in Morocco has extensively discussed the *leff* (sic) as a kind of alliance system in contrast to the "pure segmentary system" of patrilineal descent groups.[2] Studying the dynamic interplay of these conceptually distinguishable forms of organization in a village like Barouk would be an interesting task.

---

[1] Speaking of some political allies as "clans" of one's family was only one of the ways that kinship and political association were intermingled. Another was the practice of estimating the size of a family by the number of voters in it, a practice found in other parts of Lebanese society also. These patterns of speech may be retentions from a period when political statuses and roles depended on family ties, as was discussed. Alternatively, they may indicate that kinship organization is more fluid than some discussions of it have indicated.

[2] The classic statement of *laff* organization is Montagne (1930); Gellner (1969) takes an opposing view. A succinct description of the controversy and a thoughtful application of both theories can be found in Rassam Vinogradov (1974). See also Seddon (1973) for another example of a "tribe" which apparently used both forms of organization.

Still another extension one might make from this monograph would be doing research in a Lebanese urban setting, particularly in one of the suburbs of Beirut. Recent research in such suburbs[3] indicates that sectarian feeling often increases as rural immigrants move in. The residential pattern usually found in "plural" villages is repeated here on a larger scale, with one whole suburb populated predominately by one sect, another suburb "belonging to" another one, and so on. (Analogous but not isometric conditions prevail with regard to the residential patterning of socio-economic classes.)

Since most of the suburbs have sufficient facilities to provide the necessities of daily life (food stores, water, entertainment, etc.), and since rural immigrants usually maintain some ties with their villages of origin anyway, people living in the suburbs tend not to develop the intricate, cross-cutting web of relationships with members of other sects, factions, and classes that are found in many, if not all, Lebanese villages. The lack of such relationships thus makes the suburbs fertile ground for political discord. (And it was, in fact, exactly there that fighting exploded in April 1975, then spread to other parts of the city.) Furthermore, since the population of a given suburb tends to belong to one sect, politicians find it less necessary to appeal for cross-sectarian support and more easy to mobilize followers on religious grounds.

These general considerations offer some illumination to factors involved in the current civil war. Within the year following the spring of 1975, two major elections were scheduled in Lebanon: the first by popular vote for the next Chamber of Deputies, and the second, by those deputies for the Presidency of the republic. With both the opportunity and the motives present for political "negotiation by firepower," outsiders exploited the situation by pouring in modern weapons, money, and even troops. The crime that resulted left tens of thousands dead, more wounded and mutilated, much destruction and loss. While at the moment I am writing the news media are no longer filled with the daily deathcount from Beirut, the basic problems simmer on beneath the (somewhat effective) military occupation of most of the country by Arab (generally Syrian) peace forces.

While little can be done from here to influence the situation, it is possible to attempt clarification of what has happened–is happening–and why. Arms shipments, personnel, and direct military support from outside parties have gone to both major protagonists at different times in the war. Probably former U.S. Ambassador Godley's experience with extensive clandestine operations in Laos–where he became known as the "field marshall" during operations by the 50,000 man "secret army" financed by the CIA[4]–is not

---

[3]The work of Khuri (1972, 1975) and, even more, that of Joseph (1975) are good examples of such research.

[4]Marchetti and Marks (1974:320).

entirely foreign to the situation, either. But these factors, however akin they are to throwing gasoline on an open fire, did not create that fire. Rather, the major underlying causes are the social, economic, and political conditions that are withering the cross-cutting affiliations characteristic of Lebanese village society.[5] If Lebanon's future is not to be bloodied and burnt by more, and more violent, eruptions of social change, both the Lebanese and sympathetic outsiders must learn to deal with those conditions as they are and as they are likely to develop. Therefore humane, as well as intellectual, considerations demand that a high priority be given to research in the Lebanese suburbs.

---

[5]These remarks will be amplified and clarified in a later article on the civil war (Huxley, forthcoming).

APPENDIX 1

APPENDIX 1. QUESTIONNAIRE

Household Name:
(husband)
(wife)
(children)
(other–specify relation)

1. Sex: M F

2. Religion:
Druze layman   Druze religious specialist   Maronite   Catholic
Other (specify)

3. Age:

4. Residence in Barouk:
permanent emigrant   temporary emigrant   weekend and holiday
winter and summer   summer only   number of years

5. Level of education:
university or professional   some university or professional   vocational
secondary   some secondary   middle   some middle   elementary
some elementary   none

6. Type of elementary school:
government in Barouk   other government   private Druze
private Catholic   other private

7. Type of middle school:
government in Barouk   other government   private Druze
private Catholic   other private

8. Type of secondary school:
private   government

9. University or professional institute:
Lebanese government   Arab   other local   foreign

10. Work in Barouk:
    agriculture (own land) agriculture (partner) agriculture (laborer)
    self-employed government employee other employment none

11. Work outside Barouk:
    agriculture (own land) agriculture (partner) agriculture (laborer)
    self-employed government employee other employment none

12. Household income from:
    agriculture:
    rent of property:
    herds or herd products:
    commerce or self-employment (shoemaker, blacksmith, etc.):
    salary:
    pension:
    remittance from abroad:
    other income:
    (Is there anyone else contributing to family income?—
    check questions 10 & 11—if so, include above in proper
    category) Total:

13. Household expenditure:
    education:
    clothes:
    rent:
    medicine and health:
    food:
    entertainment:
    savings:
    (other expenditures?):
    Total:

14. Household private property: Y or N (number)
    car television sewing machine washer refrigerator oven telephone

15. Household productive property: Y or N (number)
    cow sheep goat burro truck tractor spraying equipment

16. Type and amount of owned land:
    irrigated for grapes and figs unirrigated prod. pine trees other trees
    unused other

17. Type and amount of rented land:
    categories as above and from whom do you rent it:
    type of rent for each piece:

18. Other land (type and amount):
19. Tenure of house:
    owned rented other (specify)
20. Form of house:
    all concrete stone with concrete roof stone with earth roof
    stone with tile roof other
21. How many rooms are there in the house (excluding kitchen and bathroom):
22. Bathroom: Y or N (number)
    none western turkish entry inside house entry outside house
    hot water bathtub or shower
23. Heating of house:
    heating stove using wood heating stove using fuel oil gas space heater
    kerosene space heater electric space heater fireplace central heating
    none other (specify)
24. Other buildings (location, tenure, and form):

Property Outside Barouk

25. Place (if in city, which section):
26. Type and amount of land which you own:
    irrigated for grapes and figs unirrigated prod. pine trees other trees
    unused land other
27. Type and amount of land which you rent:
    (like 17)
28. Other land:
    (like 18)
29. Tenure of house:
    (like 20 and apartment)
30. Form of house:
    (like 20 and apartment)
31. Number of rooms in house:
32. Bathroom:
    (like 22)
33. Heating:
    (like 23)
34. Other buildings:
    (like 24)

Other Economic Information

35. Do you cooperate with other people in agriculture, commerce, or other work (if yes, how and with whom):

36. In your opinion, into how many social classes can the population of Barouk be divided (what are the names of these classes):

37. Into what classes do you put yourselves:
    social class:
    economic class:

38. Who are the influential people:
    in Barouk (village):
    in the Shuf (region):

39. Are you a member of one of the following associations (if so, which?):
    cooperative   labor union   benevolent association   family association
    cultural club

Marriage

40. Was there an acquaintance between your wife and yourself before marriage; what was the basis for this acquaintance:

41. Are there families whose daughters your son can marry but whose sons you would not allow to marry your daughter (if yes, who):

42. Conversely, are there families whose sons can marry your daughters, but whose daughters your son cannot marry (if yes, who):

43. What are the things which allow you to decide who are مزاويبكم (i.e., "the people you usually marry"):

Visits

44. How many times do you (pl.) visit people because of:
    ("close affection"):
    ("sociability only"):
    ("personal vested interest"):
    ("social obligation"):

45. Within Barouk who are the three households which you (pl.) exchange visits with the most:
    (a) names:
    (b) how many times do you visit them:
    (c) what are your relations with them:
    (d) what are the reasons for these visits:

46. Within Barouk, are there people who usually visit you (pl.) but whom you do not usually visit in return?
(if yes, like 45a,b,c,d):

47. Conversely, within Barouk are there people whom you (pl.) usually visit but do not usually visit you in return?
(if yes, like 45a,b,c,d):

48. Outside Barouk, how often do you visit people because of (like 44):

49. Outside of Barouk, who are the three households which you (pl.) exchange visits with the most?

50. From outside Barouk, are there people who usually visit you (pl.) but whom you usually do not visit in return?
(if yes, like 45a,b,c,d):

51. Outside Barouk, are there people whom you (pl.) usually visit but who do not usually visit you in return?
(if yes, like 45a,b,c,d):

52. What are the things which permit you to decide who are the people with whom you exchange visits:

53. Have you travelled or lived outside Lebanon; if so:
where:
when:

APPENDIX 2

Appendix 2*a*
Cochran's Q Test for Significant Difference between Druze and Christian Subgroups' Fixed Sorts and Their Analyzed Free Sorts (as shown by the diameter diagram) for "Persons between Whom There is Economic Exchange"

Card Number	Fixed Sorts: Druze					Fixed Sorts: Christian			Free Sorts	L_i D	L_i C	L_i^2 D	L_i^2 C
1.	0	0	0	0	0	0	0	0	0	0	0	0	0
2.	1	1	1	1	1	1	1	1	1	6	4	36	16
3.	1	1	1	1	1	1	1	1	1	6	4	36	16
4.	0	1	0	0	0	0	0	0	0	1	0	1	0
5.	1	0	0	0	0	0	0	0	0	1	0	1	0
6.	0	0	0	0	0	1	0	0	0	0	1	0	1
7.	0	0	0	0	1	0	0	0	0	1	0	1	0
8.	1	0	0	0	0	0	0	0	0	1	0	1	0
9.	1	0	0	0	0	0	0	1	0	1	1	1	1
10.	1	1	1	1	1	1	1	1	1	6	4	36	16
11.	1	0	0	0	0	0	0	0	0	1	0	1	0
12.	0	0	0	1	0	0	0	1	0	1	1	1	1
13.	1	0	0	0	0	0	0	1	0	1	1	1	1
14.	1	0	0	0	1	1	1	1	0	2	3	4	9
15.	1	0	0	0	0	0	0	1	0	1	1	1	1
16.	1	1	0	0	0	1	0	1	0	2	2	4	4
17.	0	0	0	0	0	0	0	0	0	0	0	0	0
18.	0	0	0	0	1	1	0	1	0	1	2	1	4
	11	5	3	4	6	7	4	10	3	32	24	129	70

$\Sigma Gj_D = 32$ $\Sigma Gj_C = 24$

$$Q_D = (6\text{-}1) \frac{(6\,[11^2+5^2+3^2+4^2+6^2+3^2]\ \text{-}32^2)}{6(32)\text{-}129} = 21.59$$

$$Q_C = (4\text{-}1) \frac{(4\,[7^2+4^2+10^2+3^2]\ \text{-}24^2)}{4(24)\text{-}70} = 13.85$$

H_o = no significant difference between Druze and Christian subgroups' fixed sorts and their analyzed free sorts

$df_D = 6\text{-}1 = 5$
$p(\chi^2 \geqslant 11.07) = .05$
$21.59 > 11.07$

$df_C = 4\text{-}1 = 3$
$p(\chi^2 \geqslant 7.82) = .05$
$13.85 > 7.82$

Therefore, H_o *can* be rejected.

Appendix 2*b*

Cochran's Q Test for Significant Difference between Druze and Christian (without upper class) Subgroups' Fixed Sorts and Their Analyzed Free Sorts (as shown by the diameter diagram) for "Persons between Whom There is Economic Exchange"

Card Number	Fixed Sorts						Free Sorts	L_i		L_i^2	
	Druze				Christian			D	C	D	C
1.	0	0	0	0	0	0	0	0	0	0	0
2.	1	1	1	1	1	1	1	5	3	25	9
3.	1	1	1	1	1	1	1	5	3	25	9
4.	1	0	0	0	0	0	0	1	0	1	0
5.	0	0	0	0	0	0	0	0	0	0	0
6.	0	0	0	0	1	0	0	0	1	0	1
7.	0	0	0	1	1	0	0	1	1	1	1
8.	0	0	0	0	0	0	0	0	0	0	0
9.	0	0	0	0	0	0	0	0	0	0	0
10.	1	1	1	1	1	1	1	5	3	25	9
11.	0	0	0	0	0	0	0	0	0	0	0
12.	0	0	1	0	0	0	0	1	0	1	0
13.	0	0	0	0	0	0	0	0	0	0	0
14.	0	0	0	1	1	1	0	1	2	1	4
15.	0	0	0	0	0	0	0	0	0	0	0
16.	1	0	0	0	1	0	0	1	1	1	1
17.	0	0	0	0	0	0	0	0	0	0	0
18.	0	0	0	1	1	0	0	1	1	1	1
	5	3	4	6	7	4	3	21	14	81	30

$\Sigma\, Gj_D = 21$ $\Sigma\, Gj_C = 14$

$$Q_D = (5\text{-}1)\ \frac{(5\ [5^2+3^2+4^2+6^2+3^2]\ \text{-}21^2)}{5(21)\text{-}81} = 5.67$$

$$Q_C = (3\text{-}1)\ \frac{(3\ [7^2+4^2+3^2)\ \text{-}14^2)}{3(14)\text{-}30} = 4.33$$

H_o = no significant difference between Druze and Christian (without upper class) subgroups' fixed sorts and their analyzed free sorts

$df_D = 5\text{-}1 = 4$
$p(\chi^2 \geqslant 9.49) = .05$
$5.67 < 9.49$

$df_C = 3\text{-}1 = 2$
$p(\chi^2 \geqslant 5.99) = .05$
$4.33 < 5.99$

Therefore, H_o can *not* be rejected.

Appendix 2*c*

Cochran's Q Test for Significant Difference between Druze and Christian Subgroups' Fixed Sorts and Their Analyzed Free Sorts (as shown by the diameter diagram) for "Persons between Whom There is Political Exchange"

Card Number	Fixed Sorts								Free Sorts	L_i		L_i^2	
	Druze					Christian				D	C	D	C
1.	0	0	0	0	0	1	0	0	0	0	1	0	1
2.	0	0	0	0	0	0	0	1	0	0	1	0	1
3.	0	0	0	0	1	0	0	1	0	1	1	1	1
4.	0	0	0	0	0	1	0	0	0	0	1	0	1
5.	1	1	1	1	1	1	1	1	1	6	4	36	16
6.	0	0	0	0	0	0	0	0	0	0	0	0	0
7.	1	1	1	0	1	1	0	0	1	5	2	25	4
8.	1	1	1	1	1	1	1	1	1	6	4	36	16
9.	1	1	1	1	0	0	1	1	1	5	3	25	9
10.	0	0	0	0	0	0	0	1	0	0	1	0	1
11.	1	1	1	1	1	1	0	1	1	6	3	36	9
12.	1	0	1	1	1	0	1	1	1	5	3	25	9
13.	1	0	1	1	1	1	0	1	1	5	3	25	9
14.	0	0	0	0	0	0	0	0	0	0	0	0	0
15.	1	1	1	1	1	0	1	1	1	6	3	36	9
16.	1	0	1	1	0	0	0	0	1	4	1	16	1
17.	0	0	0	0	0	1	0	0	0	0	1	0	1
18.	0	0	0	0	0	0	0	0	0	0	0	0	0
	9	6	9	8	8	8	5	10	9	49	32	262	87

$\Sigma\, Gj_D = 49$ $\qquad$ $\Sigma\, Gj_C = 32$

$$Q_D = (6\text{-}1)\ \frac{(6\,[9^2+6^2+9^2+8^2+8^2+9^2]\ \text{-}49^2)}{6(49)\text{-}262} = 6.41$$

$$Q_C = (4\text{-}1)\ \frac{(4\,[8^2+5^2+10^2+9^2]\ \text{-}32^2)}{4(32)\text{-}87} = 4.10$$

H_o = no significant difference between Druze and Christian subgroups' fixed sorts and their analyzed free sorts

$df_D = 6\text{-}1 = 5$
$p(\chi^2 \geqslant 11.07) = .05$
$6.41 < 11.07$

$df_C = 4\text{-}1 = 3$
$p(\chi^2 \geqslant 7.82) = .05$
$4.10 < 7.82$

Therefore, H_o can *not* be rejected.

Appendix 2*d*
Cochran's Q Test for Significant Difference between Druze and Christian Subgroups' Fixed Sorts
and Their Analyzed Free Sorts (as shown by the diameter diagram) for "Persons between Whom There is Mutual Social Exchange"

Card Number	Fixed Sorts								Free Sorts	L_i		L_i^2	
	Druze					Christian				D	C	D	C
1.	1	1	1	1	1	1	1	1	1	6	4	36	16
2.	0	0	0	0	0	0	0	0	0	0	0	0	0
3.	0	0	0	0	0	0	0	0	0	0	0	0	0
4.	1	0	1	1	1	1	0	0	1	5	2	25	4
5.	0	0	0	0	0	0	0	1	0	0	1	0	1
6.	1	1	0	1	0	1	1	1	1	4	4	16	16
7.	0	0	0	0	0	0	0	1	0	0	1	0	1
8.	0	0	0	0	0	0	0	1	0	0	1	0	1
9.	0	0	0	0	0	0	0	0	0	0	0	0	0
10.	0	0	0	0	0	0	0	0	0	0	0	0	0
11.	0	0	0	0	1	0	0	0	0	1	0	1	0
12.	0	0	0	0	0	0	0	0	0	0	0	0	0
13.	0	0	0	0	0	0	0	0	0	0	0	0	0
14.	0	0	0	0	1	0	0	0	0	1	0	1	0
15.	0	0	0	0	0	0	0	1	0	0	1	0	1
16.	0	0	0	0	0	0	0	0	0	0	0	0	0
17.	1	1	1	1	1	1	1	1	1	6	4	36	16
18.	1	1	0	0	1	0	0	0	0	3	0	9	0
	5	4	3	4	6	4	3	7	4	26	18	124	56

$\Sigma Gj_D = 26$ $\Sigma Gj_C = 18$

$$Q_D = (6\text{-}1)\frac{(6\,[5^2+4^2+3^2+4^2+6^2+4^2]\ \text{-}26^2)}{6(26)\text{-}124} = 5.00$$

$$Q_C = (4\text{-}1)\frac{(4\,[4^2+3^2+7^2+4^2]\ \text{-}18^2)}{4(18)\text{-}56} = 6.75$$

H_o = no significant difference between Druze and Christian subgroups' fixed sorts and their analyzed free sorts

$df_D = 6\text{-}1 = 5$
$p(\chi^2 \geqslant 11.07) = .05$
$5.00 < 11.07$

$df_C = 4\text{-}1 = 3$
$p(\chi^2 \geqslant 7.82) = .05$
$6.75 < 7.82$

Therefore, H_o can *not* be rejected.

Appendix 2*e*
Cochran's Q Test for Significant Difference between Druze and Christian Subgroups' Fixed Sorts and Their Analyzed Free Sorts (as shown by the diameter diagram) for "Higher Statuses" among "Persons between Whom There is Economic Exchange"

Card Number	Fixed Sorts								Free Sorts	L_i		L_i^2	
	Druze					Christian				D	C	D	C
1.	0	0	0	0	0	0	0	0	0	0	0	0	0
2.	0	0	0	0	0	0	0	1	0	0	1	0	1
3.	0	0	0	0	0	0	0	0	0	0	0	0	0
4.	0	1	0	0	0	0	0	0	0	1	0	1	0
5.	0	0	0	0	0	0	0	0	0	0	0	0	0
6.	0	0	0	0	0	0	0	0	0	0	0	0	0
7.	0	0	0	1	0	1	0	0	0	1	1	1	1
8.	0	0	0	0	0	0	0	0	0	0	0	0	0
9.	0	0	0	0	0	0	0	0	0	0	0	0	0
10.	1	1	0	0	0	0	1	0	1	3	2	9	4
11.	0	0	0	0	0	0	0	0	0	0	0	0	0
12.	0	0	0	0	0	0	0	0	0	0	0	0	0
13.	0	0	0	0	0	0	0	0	0	0	0	0	0
14.	0	0	0	0	0	0	1	0	0	0	1	0	1
15.	0	0	0	0	0	0	0	0	0	0	0	0	0
16.	0	1	0	0	0	0	0	0	0	1	0	1	0
17.	0	0	0	0	0	0	0	0	0	0	0	0	0
18.	0	0	0	1	0	0	0	0	0	1	0	1	0
	1	3	0	2	0	2	2	0	1	7	5	13	7

$\Sigma Gj_D = 7$ $\Sigma Gj_C = 5$

$$Q_D = (6\text{-}1)\frac{(6\,[1^2+3^2+0^2+2^2+0^2+1^2]\,-7^2)}{6(7)-13} = 7.07$$

$$Q_C = (4\text{-}1)\frac{(4\,[2^2+2^2+0^2+1^2]\,-5^2)}{4(5)-7} = 2.54$$

H_o = no significant difference between Druze and Christian subgroups' fixed sorts and their analyzed free sorts

$df_D = 6\text{-}1 = 5$
$p(\chi^2 \geqslant 11.07) = .05$
$7.07 < 11.07$

$df_C = 4\text{-}1 = 3$
$p(\chi^2 \geqslant 7.82) = .05$
$3.67 < 7.82$

Therefore, H_o can *not* be rejected.

Appendix 2*f*

Cochran's Q Test for Significant Difference between Druze and Christian Subgroups' Fixed Sorts and Their Analyzed Free Sorts (as shown by the diameter diagram) for "Lower Statuses" among "Persons between Whom There is Economic Exchange"

Card Number	Fixed Sorts								Free Sorts	L_i		L_i^2	
	Druze					Christian				D	C	D	C
1.	0	0	0	0	0	0	0	0	0	0	0	0	0
2.	1	1	0	1	0	0	1	0	1	4	2	16	4
3.	1	1	0	1	0	1	1	1	1	4	4	16	16
4.	0	0	0	0	0	0	0	0	0	0	0	0	0
5.	0	0	0	0	0	0	0	0	0	0	0	0	0
6.	0	0	0	0	0	0	0	0	0	0	0	0	0
7.	0	0	0	0	0	0	0	0	0	0	0	0	0
8.	0	0	0	0	0	0	0	0	0	0	0	0	0
9.	0	0	0	0	0	0	0	1	0	0	1	0	1
10.	0	0	0	1	0	0	0	0	0	1	0	1	0
11.	0	0	0	0	0	0	0	0	0	0	0	0	0
12.	0	0	0	0	0	0	0	1	0	0	1	0	1
13.	0	0	0	0	0	0	0	1	0	0	1	0	1
14.	0	0	0	1	0	0	0	0	0	1	0	1	0
15.	0	0	0	0	0	0	0	1	0	0	1	0	1
16.	0	0	0	0	0	0	0	1	0	0	1	0	1
17.	0	0	0	0	0	0	0	0	0	0	0	0	0
18.	0	0	0	0	0	0	0	0	0	0	0	0	0
	2	2	0	4	0	1	2	6	2	10	11	34	25

$\Sigma Gj_D = 10$ $\Sigma Gj_C = 11$

$$Q_D = (6\text{-}1)\ \frac{(6\ [2^2+2^2+0^2+4^2+0^2+2^2]\ \text{-}10^2)}{6(10)\text{-}34} = 13.05$$

$$Q_C = (4\text{-}1)\ \frac{(4\ [1^2+2^2+6^2+2^2]\ \text{-}11^2)}{4(11)\text{-}25} = 9.32$$

H_o = no significant difference between Druze and Christian subgroups' fixed sorts and their analyzed free sorts

$df_D = 6\text{-}1 = 5$
$p(\chi^2 \geqslant 11.07) = .05$
$13.08 > 11.07$

$df_C = 4\text{-}1 = 3$
$p(\chi^2 \geqslant 7.82) = .05$
$9.32 > 7.82$

Therefore, H_o *can* be rejected.

Appendix 2*g*

Cochran's Q Test for Significant Difference between Druze and Christian (without upper class) Subgroups' Fixed Sorts and Their Analyzed Free Sorts (as shown by the diameter diagram) for "Lower Statuses" among "Persons between Whom There is Economic Exchange"

Card Number	Fixed Sorts						Free Sorts	L_i		L_i^2	
	Druze				Christian			D	C	D	C
1.	0	0	0	0	0	0	0	0	0	0	0
2.	1	1	0	1	0	1	1	4	2	16	4
3.	1	1	0	1	1	1	1	4	3	16	9
4.	0	0	0	0	0	0	0	0	0	0	0
5.	0	0	0	0	0	0	0	0	0	0	0
6.	0	0	0	0	0	0	0	0	0	0	0
7.	0	0	0	0	0	0	0	0	0	0	0
8.	0	0	0	0	0	0	0	0	0	0	0
9.	0	0	0	0	0	0	0	0	0	0	0
10.	0	0	0	1	0	0	0	1	0	1	0
11.	0	0	0	0	0	0	0	0	0	0	0
12.	0	0	0	0	0	0	0	0	0	0	0
13.	0	0	0	0	0	0	0	0	0	0	0
14.	0	0	0	1	0	0	0	1	0	1	0
15.	0	0	0	0	0	0	0	0	0	0	0
16.	0	0	0	0	0	0	0	0	0	0	0
17.	0	0	0	0	0	0	0	0	0	0	0
18.	0	0	0	0	0	0	0	0	0	0	0
	2	2	0	4	1	2	2	10	5	34	13

$\Sigma\, Gj_D = 10$ $\Sigma\, Gj_C = 11$

$$Q_D = (5\text{-}1)\ \frac{(5\,[2^2+2^2+0^2+4^2+2^2]\ \text{-}10^2)}{5(10)\text{-}34} = 10.00$$

$$Q_C = (3\text{-}1)\ \frac{(3\,[1^2+2^2+2^2]\ \text{-}5^2)}{3(5)\text{-}13} = 2.00$$

H_o = no significant difference between Druze and Christian (without upper class) subgroups' fixed sorts and their analyzed free sorts

$df_D = 5\text{-}1 = 4$
$p(\chi^2 \geqslant 9.49) = .05$
$10.00 > 9.49$

$df_C = 3\text{-}1 = 2$
$p(\chi^2 \geqslant 5.99) = .05$
$2.00 < 5.99$

Therefore, H_o *can* be rejected for the Druze subgroup (without upper class) but *not* for the Christian one (without upper class).

Appendix 2*h*

Cochran's Q Test for Significant Difference between Druze and Christian Subgroups' Fixed Sorts and Their Analyzed Free Sorts (as shown by the diameter diagram) for "Higher Statuses" among "Persons between Whom There is Political Exchange"

Card Number	Fixed Sorts								Free Sorts	L_i		L_i^2	
	Druze					Christian				D	C	D	C
1.	0	0	0	0	0	0	0	0	0	0	0	0	0
2.	0	0	0	0	0	0	0	0	0	0	0	0	0
3.	0	0	0	0	0	0	0	0	0	0	0	0	0
4.	0	0	0	0	0	0	0	0	0	0	0	0	0
5.	1	1	1	1	1	1	1	1	1	6	4	36	16
6.	0	0	0	0	0	0	0	0	0	0	0	0	0
7.	1	0	0	0	1	1	0	0	1	3	2	9	4
8.	1	1	1	1	1	1	1	1	1	6	4	36	16
9.	0	0	1	0	0	0	1	0	0	1	1	1	1
10.	0	0	0	0	0	0	0	0	0	0	0	0	0
11.	0	1	1	0	0	1	0	0	0	2	1	4	1
12.	0	0	0	0	0	0	0	0	0	0	0	0	0
13.	0	0	0	0	0	0	0	0	0	0	0	0	0
14.	0	0	0	0	0	0	0	0	0	0	0	0	0
15.	0	0	0	0	0	0	0	0	0	0	0	0	0
16.	1	0	1	1	0	0	0	0	1	4	1	16	1
17.	0	0	0	0	0	0	0	0	0	0	0	0	0
18.	0	0	0	0	0	0	0	0	0	0	0	0	0
	4	3	5	3	3	4	3	2	4	22	13	102	39

$\Sigma Gj_D = 22$ $\Sigma Gj_C = 13$

$$Q_D = (6\text{-}1) \frac{(6\ [4^2+3^2+5^2+3^2+3^2+4^2)\ \text{-}22^2)}{6(22)\text{-}102} = 3.33$$

$$Q_C = (4\text{-}1) \frac{(4\ [4^2+3^2+2^2+4^2)\ \text{-}13^2)}{4(13)\text{-}39} = 2.54$$

H_o = no significant difference between Druze and Christian subgroups' fixed sorts and their analyzed free sorts

$df_D = 6\text{-}1 = 5$
$p(\chi^2 \geqslant 11.07) = .05$
$3.33 < 11.07$

$df_C = 4\text{-}1 = 3$
$p(\chi^2 \geqslant 7.82) = .05$
$2.54 < 7.82$

Therefore, H_o can *not* be rejected.

Appendix 2*i*

Cochran's Q Test for Significant Difference between Druze and Christian Subgroups' Fixed Sorts and Their Analyzed Free Sorts (as shown by the diameter diagram) for "Lower Statuses" among "Persons between Whom There is Political Exchange"

Card Number	Fixed Sorts								Free Sorts	L_i		L_i^2	
	Druze					Christian				D	C	D	C
1.	0	0	0	0	0	1	0	0	0	0	1	0	1
2.	0	0	0	0	0	0	0	0	0	0	0	0	0
3.	0	0	0	0	0	0	0	0	0	0	0	0	0
4.	0	0	0	0	0	1	0	0	0	0	1	0	1
5.	0	0	0	0	0	0	0	0	0	0	0	0	0
6.	0	0	0	0	0	0	0	0	0	0	0	0	0
7.	0	1	1	0	0	0	0	0	0	2	0	4	0
8.	0	0	0	0	0	0	0	0	0	0	0	0	0
9.	1	1	0	1	0	0	0	1	1	4	2	16	4
10.	0	0	0	0	0	0	0	0	0	0	0	0	0
11.	1	0	0	1	0	0	0	1	1	3	2	9	4
12.	1	0	1	1	1	0	1	1	1	5	3	25	9
13.	1	0	1	1	1	1	0	1	1	5	3	25	9
14.	0	0	0	0	0	0	0	0	0	0	0	0	0
15.	1	1	1	1	1	0	1	1	1	6	3	36	9
16.	0	0	0	0	0	0	0	0	0	0	0	0	0
17.	0	0	0	0	0	1	0	0	0	0	1	0	1
18.	0	0	0	0	0	0	0	0	0	0	0	0	0
	5	3	4	5	3	4	2	5	5	25	16	115	38

$\Sigma Gj_D = 25$ $\Sigma Gj_C = 16$

$$Q_D = (6\text{-}1) \frac{(6\,[5^2+3^2+4^2+5^2+3^2+5^2]\ \text{-}25^2)}{6(25)\text{-}115} = 4.14$$

$$Q_C = (4\text{-}1) \frac{(4\,[4^2+2^2+5^2+5^2]\ \text{-}16^2)}{4(16)\text{-}38} = 2.77$$

H_o = no significant difference between Druze and Christian subgroups' fixed sorts and their analyzed free sorts

$df_D = 6\text{-}1 = 5$
$p(\chi^2 \geqslant 11.07) = .05$
$4.14 < 11.07$

$df_C = 4\text{-}1 = 3$
$p(\chi^2 \geqslant 7.82) = .05$
$2.77 < 7.82$

Therefore, H_o can *not* be rejected.

APPENDIX 3

Appendix 3*a*

Cochran's Q Test for Significant Difference between Yazbaki and Junblāṭṭi subgroups' Fixed Sorts and Their Analyzed Free Sorts (as shown by the diameter diagram) for "Persons between Whom There is Economic Exchange"

Card Number	Fixed Sorts								Free Sorts	L_i		L_i^2	
	Yazbaki				Junblāṭṭi					Y	J	Y	J
1.	0	0	0	0	0	0	0	0	0	0	0	0	0
2.	1	1	1	1	1	1	1	1	1	5	5	25	25
3.	1	1	1	1	1	1	1	1	1	5	5	25	25
4.	0	1	0	0	0	0	0	0	0	1	0	1	0
5.	0	0	0	0	0	0	0	1	0	0	1	0	1
6.	0	0	0	0	1	0	0	0	0	0	1	0	1
7.	1	0	0	0	1	0	0	0	0	1	1	1	1
8.	0	0	0	0	0	0	0	1	0	0	1	0	1
9.	0	0	0	1	0	0	0	1	0	1	1	1	1
10.	1	1	1	1	0	1	1	1	1	5	4	25	16
11.	0	0	0	0	0	0	0	1	0	0	1	0	1
12.	0	0	0	1	0	0	1	0	0	1	1	1	1
13.	0	0	0	1	0	0	0	1	0	1	1	1	1
14.	1	0	0	1	1	1	0	1	0	2	3	4	9
15.	0	0	0	1	0	0	0	1	0	1	1	1	1
16.	0	1	0	1	1	0	0	1	0	2	2	4	4
17.	0	0	0	0	0	0	0	0	0	0	0	0	0
18.	1	0	0	1	1	0	0	0	0	2	1	4	1
	6	5	3	10	7	4	4	11	3	27	29	93	89

$\Sigma Gj_Y = 27$ $\Sigma Gj_J = 29$

$$Q_Y = (5\text{-}1)\ \frac{(5\ [6^2+5^2+3^2+10^2+3^2]\ -27^2)}{5(27)\text{-}93} = 15.81$$

$$Q_J = (5\text{-}1)\ \frac{(5\ [7^2+4^2+4^2+11^2+3^2]\ -29^2)}{5(29)\text{-}89} = 15.29$$

H_o = no significant difference between Yazbaki and Junblāṭṭi subgroups' fixed sorts and their analyzed free sorts

$df_Y = 5\text{-}1 = 4$
$p(\chi^2 \geqslant 9.49) = .05$
$15.81 > 9.49$

$df_J = 5\text{-}1 = 4$
$p(\chi^2 \geqslant 9.49) = .05$
$15.29 > 9.49$

Therefore, H_o *can* be rejected.

Appendix 3*b*

Cochran's Q Test for Significant Difference between Yazbaki and Junblāṭṭi (without upper class) Subgroups' Fixed Sorts and Their Analyzed Free Sorts (as shown by the diameter diagram) for "Persons between Whom There is Economic Exchange"

Card Number	Fixed Sorts						Free Sorts	L_i		L_i^2	
	Yazbaki			Junblāṭṭi				Y	J	Y	J
1.	0	0	0	0	0	0	0	0	0	0	0
2.	1	1	1	1	1	1	1	4	4	16	16
3.	1	1	1	1	1	1	1	4	4	16	16
4.	0	1	0	0	0	0	0	1	0	1	0
5.	0	0	0	0	0	0	0	0	0	0	0
6.	0	0	0	1	0	0	0	0	1	0	1
7.	1	0	0	1	0	0	0	1	1	1	1
8.	0	0	0	0	0	0	0	0	0	0	0
9.	0	0	0	0	0	0	0	0	0	0	0
10.	1	1	1	0	1	1	1	4	3	16	9
11.	0	0	0	0	0	0	0	0	0	0	0
12.	0	0	0	0	0	1	0	0	1	0	1
13.	0	0	0	0	0	0	0	0	0	0	0
14.	1	0	0	1	1	0	0	1	2	1	4
15.	0	0	0	0	0	0	0	0	0	0	0
16.	0	1	0	1	0	0	0	1	1	1	1
17.	0	0	0	0	0	0	0	0	0	0	0
18.	1	0	0	1	0	0	0	1	1	1	1
	6	5	3	7	4	4	3	27	29	53	52

$\Sigma Gj_Y = 27$ $\Sigma Gj_J = 29$

$$Q_Y = (4\text{-}1) \frac{(4\ [6^2+5^2+3^2+3^2)\ \text{-}27^2)}{4(27)\text{-}53} = 5.40$$

$$Q_J = (4\text{-}1) \frac{(4\ [7^2+4^2+4^2+3^2]\ \text{-}29^2)}{4(29)\text{-}52} = 5.40$$

H_o = no significant difference between Yazbaki and Junblāṭṭi (without upper class) subgroups' fixed sorts and their analyzed free sorts

$df_Y = 4\text{-}1 = 3$
$p(\chi^2 \geqslant 7.82) = .05$
$5.40 < 7.82$

$df_J = 4\text{-}1 = 3$
$p(\chi^2 \geqslant 7.82) = .05$
$5.40 < 7.82$

Therefore, H_o can *not* be rejected.

Appendix 3*c*
Cochran's Q Test for Significant Difference between Yazbaki and Junblāṭṭi Subgroups' Fixed Sorts and Their Analyzed Free Sorts (as shown by the diameter diagram) for "Persons between Whom There is Political Exchange"

Card Number	Fixed Sorts								Free Sorts	L_i		L_i^2	
	Yazbaki				Junblāṭṭi					Y	J	Y	J
1.	0	0	0	0	1	0	0	0	0	0	1	0	1
2.	0	0	0	1	0	0	0	0	0	1	0	1	0
3.	0	0	0	1	0	0	0	1	0	1	1	1	1
4.	0	0	0	0	1	0	0	0	0	0	1	0	1
5.	1	1	1	1	1	1	1	1	1	5	5	25	25
6.	0	0	0	0	0	0	0	0	0	0	0	0	0
7.	0	1	1	0	1	0	1	1	1	3	4	9	16
8.	1	1	1	1	1	1	1	1	1	5	5	25	25
9.	1	1	1	1	0	1	1	0	1	5	3	25	9
10.	0	0	0	1	0	0	0	0	0	1	0	1	0
11.	1	1	1	1	1	0	1	1	1	5	4	25	16
12.	1	0	1	1	0	1	1	1	1	4	4	16	16
13.	1	0	1	1	1	0	1	1	1	4	4	16	16
14.	0	0	0	0	0	0	0	0	0	0	0	0	0
15.	1	1	1	1	0	1	1	1	1	5	4	25	16
16.	1	0	1	0	0	0	1	0	1	3	2	9	4
17.	0	0	0	0	1	0	0	0	0	0	1	0	1
18.	0	0	0	0	0	0	0	0	0	0	0	0	0
	8	6	9	10	8	5	9	8	9	42	39	178	147

$\Sigma\, Gj_Y = 42$ $\Sigma\, Gj_J = 39$

$$Q_Y = (5\text{-}1)\ \frac{(5\ [8^2+6^2+9^2+10^2+9^2]\ \text{-}42^2)}{5(42)\text{-}178} = 5.75$$

$$Q_J = (5\text{-}1)\ \frac{(5\ [8^2+5^2+9^2+8^2+9^2]\ \text{-}39^2)}{5(39)\text{-}147} = 4.50$$

H_O = no significant difference between Yazbaki and Junblāṭṭi subgroups' fixed sorts and their analyzed free sorts

$df_Y = 5\text{-}1 = 4$
$p(\chi^2 \geqslant 9.49) = .05$
$5.75 < 9.49$

$df_J = 5\text{-}1 = 4$
$p(\chi^2 \geqslant 9.49) = .05$
$4.50 < 9.49$

Therefore, H_O can *not* be rejected.

Appendix 3*d*
Cochran's Q Test for Significant Difference between Yazbaki and Junblāṭṭi Subgroups' Fixed Sorts and Their Analyzed Free Sorts (as shown by the diameter diagram) for "Persons between Whom There is Mutual Social Exchange"

Card Number	Fixed Sorts								Free Sorts	L_i		L_i^2	
	Yazbaki				Junblāṭṭi					Y	J	Y	J
1.	1	1	1	1	1	1	1	1	1	5	5	25	25
2.	0	0	0	0	0	0	0	0	0	0	0	0	0
3.	0	0	0	0	0	0	0	0	0	0	0	0	0
4.	1	0	1	0	0	1	1	1	1	3	4	9	16
5.	0	0	0	1	0	0	0	0	0	1	0	1	0
6.	1	1	0	1	1	1	1	0	1	4	4	16	16
7.	0	0	0	1	0	0	0	0	0	1	0	1	0
8.	0	0	0	1	0	0	0	0	0	1	0	1	0
9.	0	0	0	0	0	0	0	0	0	0	0	0	0
10.	0	0	0	0	0	0	0	0	0	0	0	0	0
11.	0	0	0	0	0	0	0	1	0	0	1	0	1
12.	0	0	0	0	0	0	0	0	0	0	0	0	0
13.	0	0	0	0	0	0	0	0	0	0	0	0	0
14.	0	0	0	0	0	0	0	1	0	0	1	0	1
15.	0	0	0	1	0	0	0	0	0	1	0	1	0
16.	0	0	0	0	0	0	0	0	0	0	0	0	0
17.	1	1	1	1	1	1	1	1	1	5	5	25	25
18.	0	1	0	0	0	0	1	1	0	1	2	1	4
	4	4	3	7	3	4	5	6	4	22	22	80	88

$\Sigma Gj_Y = 22$

$\Sigma Gj_J = 22$

$$Q_Y = (5\text{-}1) \frac{(5\,[4^2+4^2+3^2+7^2+4^2]\ \text{-}22^2)}{5(22)\text{-}80} = 6.13$$

$$Q_J = (5\text{-}1) \frac{(5\,[3^2+4^2+5^2+6^2+4^2]\ \text{-}22^2)}{5(22)\text{-}88} = 4.73$$

H_o = no significant difference between Yazbaki and Junblāṭṭi subgroups' fixed sorts and their analyzed free sorts

$df_Y = 5\text{-}1 = 4$
$p(\chi^2 \geqslant 9.49) = .05$
$6.13 < 9.49$

$df_J = 5\text{-}1 = 4$
$p(\chi^2 \geqslant 9.49) = .05$
$4.73 < 9.49$

Therefore, H_o can *not* be rejected.

Appendix 3*e*

Cochran's Q Test for Significant Difference between Yazbaki and Junblāṭṭi Subgroups' Fixed Sorts and Their Analyzed Free Sorts (as shown by the diameter diagram) for "Higher Statuses" among "Persons between Whom There is Economic Exchange"

Card Number	Fixed Sorts								Free Sorts	L_i		L_i^2	
	Yazbaki				Junblāṭṭi					Y	J	Y	J
1.	0	0	0	0	0	0	0	0	0	0	0	0	0
2.	0	0	0	0	1	0	0	0	0	0	1	0	1
3.	0	0	0	0	0	0	0	0	0	0	0	0	0
4.	0	1	0	0	0	0	0	0	0	1	0	1	0
5.	0	0	0	0	0	0	0	0	0	0	0	0	0
6.	0	0	0	0	0	0	0	0	0	0	0	0	0
7.	1	0	0	0	1	0	0	0	0	1	1	1	1
8.	0	0	0	0	0	0	0	0	0	0	0	0	0
9.	0	0	0	0	0	0	0	0	0	0	0	0	0
10.	0	1	1	0	0	1	0	0	1	3	2	9	4
11.	0	0	0	0	0	0	0	0	0	0	0	0	0
12.	0	0	0	0	0	0	0	0	0	0	0	0	0
13.	0	0	0	0	0	0	0	0	0	0	0	0	0
14.	0	0	0	0	0	1	0	0	0	0	1	0	1
15.	0	0	0	0	0	0	0	0	0	0	0	0	0
16.	0	1	0	0	0	0	0	0	0	1	0	1	0
17.	0	0	0	0	0	0	0	0	0	0	0	0	0
18.	1	0	0	0	0	0	0	0	0	1	0	1	0
	2	3	1	0	2	2	0	0	1	7	5	13	7

$\Sigma Gj_Y = 7$ $\Sigma Gj_J = 5$

$$Q_Y = (5\text{-}1)\ \frac{(5\ [2^2+3^2+1^2+0^2+1^2]\ -7^2)}{5(7)\text{-}13} = 4.73$$

$$Q_J = (5\text{-}1)\ \frac{(5\ [2^2+2^2+0^2+0^2+1^2]\ -5^2)}{5(5)\text{-}7} = 4.44$$

H_o = no significant difference between Yazbaki and Junblāṭṭi subgroups' fixed sorts and their analyzed free sorts

$df_y = 5\text{-}1 = 4$
$p(\chi^2 \geqslant 9.49) = .05$
$4.73 < 9.49$

$df_J = 5\text{-}1 = 4$
$p(\chi^2 \geqslant 9.49) = .05$
$4.44 < 9.49$

Therefore, H_o can *not* be rejected.

Appendix 3*f*

Cochran's Q Test for Significant Difference between Yazbaki and Junblāṭṭi Subgroups' Fixed Sorts and Their Analyzed Free Sorts (as shown by the diameter diagram) for "Lower Statuses" among "Persons between Whom There is Economic Exchange"

Card Number	Fixed Sorts: Yazbaki				Fixed Sorts: Junblāṭṭi				Free Sorts	L_i Y	L_i J	L_i^2 Y	L_i^2 J
1.	0	0	0	0	0	0	0	0	0	0	0	0	0
2.	1	1	1	0	0	1	0	0	1	4	2	16	4
3.	1	1	1	1	1	1	0	0	1	5	3	25	9
4.	0	0	0	0	0	0	0	0	0	0	0	0	0
5.	0	0	0	0	0	0	0	0	0	0	0	0	0
6.	0	0	0	0	0	0	0	0	0	0	0	0	0
7.	0	0	0	0	0	0	0	0	0	0	0	0	0
8.	0	0	0	0	0	0	0	0	0	0	0	0	0
9.	0	0	0	1	0	0	0	0	0	1	0	1	0
10.	1	0	0	0	0	0	0	0	0	1	0	1	0
11.	0	0	0	0	0	0	0	0	0	0	0	0	0
12.	0	0	0	1	0	0	0	0	0	1	0	1	0
13.	0	0	0	1	0	0	0	0	0	1	0	1	0
14.	1	0	0	0	0	0	0	0	0	1	0	1	0
15.	0	0	0	1	0	0	0	0	0	1	0	1	0
16.	0	0	0	1	0	0	0	0	0	1	0	1	0
17.	0	0	0	0	0	0	0	0	0	0	0	0	0
18.	0	0	0	0	0	0	0	0	0	0	0	0	0
	4	2	2	6	1	2	0	0	2	16	5	48	13

$\Sigma\, Gj_Y = 16$ $\Sigma\, Gj_J = 5$

$$Q_Y = (5\text{-}1)\ \frac{(5\ [4^2+2^2+2^2+6^2+2^2]\ -16^2)}{5(16)\text{-}48} = 8.00$$

$$Q_J = (5\text{-}1)\ \frac{(5\ [1^2+2^2+0^2+0^2+2^2]\ -5^2)}{5(5)\text{-}13} = 6.67$$

H_O = no significant difference between Yazbaki and Junblāṭṭi subgroups' fixed sorts and their analyzed free sorts

$df_Y = 5\text{-}1 = 4$
$p(\chi^2 \geqslant 9.49) = .05$
$8.00 < 9.49$

$df_J = 5\text{-}1 = 4$
$p(\chi^2 \geqslant 9.49) = .05$
$6.67 < 9.49$

Therefore, H_O can *not* be rejected.

Appendix 3*g*

Cochran's Q Test for Significant Difference between Yazbaki and Junblāṭṭi Subgroups' Fixed Sorts and Their Analyzed Free Sorts (as shown by the diameter diagram) for "Higher Statuses" among "Persons between Whom There is Political Exchange"

Card Number	Fixed Sorts								Free Sorts	L_i		L_i^2	
	Yazbaki				Junblāṭṭi					Y	J	Y	J
1.	0	0	0	0	0	0	0	0	0	0	0	0	0
2.	0	0	0	0	0	0	0	0	0	0	0	0	0
3.	0	0	0	0	0	0	0	0	0	0	0	0	0
4.	0	0	0	0	0	0	0	0	0	0	0	0	0
5.	1	1	1	1	1	1	1	1	1	5	5	25	25
6.	0	0	0	0	0	0	0	0	0	0	0	0	0
7.	0	0	1	0	1	0	0	1	1	2	3	4	9
8.	1	1	1	1	1	1	1	1	1	5	5	25	25
9.	0	0	0	0	0	1	1	0	0	0	2	0	4
10.	0	0	0	0	0	0	0	0	0	0	0	0	0
11.	0	1	0	0	1	0	1	0	0	1	2	1	4
12.	0	0	0	0	0	0	0	0	0	0	0	0	0
13.	0	0	0	0	0	0	0	0	0	0	0	0	0
14.	0	0	0	0	0	0	0	0	0	0	0	0	0
15.	0	0	0	0	0	0	0	0	0	0	0	0	0
16.	1	0	1	0	0	0	1	0	1	3	2	9	4
17.	0	0	0	0	0	0	0	0	0	0	0	0	0
18.	0	0	0	0	0	0	0	0	0	0	0	0	0
	3	3	4	2	4	3	5	3	4	16	19	64	71

$\Sigma\, Gj_Y = 16$ $\Sigma\, Gj_J = 19$

$$Q_Y = (5\text{-}1)\ \frac{(5\,[3^2+3^2+4^2+2^2+4^2]\ \text{-}16^2)}{5(16)\text{-}64} = 3.50$$

$$Q_J = (5\text{-}1)\ \frac{(5\,[4^2+3^2+5^2+3^2+4^2]\ \text{-}19^2)}{5(19)\text{-}71} = 2.33$$

H_o = no significant difference between Yazbaki and Junblāṭṭi subgroups' fixed sorts and their analyzed free sorts

$df_Y = 5\text{-}1 = 4$
$p(\chi^2 \geqslant 9.49)\ \text{-}\ .05$
$3.50 < 9.49$

$df_J = 5\text{-}1 = 4$
$p(\chi^2 \geqslant 9.49) = .05$
$2.33 < 9.49$

Therefore, H_o can *not* be rejected.

Appendix 3*h*

Cochran's Q Test for Significant Difference between Yazbaki and Junblāṭṭi Subgroups' Fixed Sorts and Their Analyzed Free Sorts (as shown by the diameter diagram) for "Lower Statuses" among "Persons between Whom There is Political Exchange"

Card Number	Fixed Sorts								Free Sorts	L_i		L_i^2	
	Yazbaki				Junblāṭṭi					Y	J	Y	J
1.	0	0	0	0	1	0	0	0	0	0	1	0	1
2.	0	0	0	0	0	0	0	0	0	0	0	0	0
3.	0	0	0	0	0	0	0	0	0	0	0	0	0
4.	0	0	0	0	1	0	0	0	0	0	1	0	1
5.	0	0	0	0	0	0	0	0	0	0	0	0	0
6.	0	0	0	0	0	0	0	0	0	0	0	0	0
7.	0	1	0	0	0	0	1	0	0	1	1	1	1
8.	0	0	0	0	0	0	0	0	0	0	0	0	0
9.	1	1	1	1	0	0	0	0	1	5	1	25	1
10.	0	0	0	0	0	0	0	0	0	0	0	0	0
11.	1	0	1	1	0	0	0	0	1	4	1	16	1
12.	1	0	1	1	0	1	1	1	1	4	4	16	16
13.	1	0	1	1	1	0	1	1	1	4	4	16	16
14.	0	0	0	0	0	0	0	0	0	0	0	0	0
15.	1	1	1	1	0	1	1	1	1	5	4	25	16
16.	0	0	0	0	0	0	0	0	0	0	0	0	0
17.	0	0	0	0	1	0	0	0	0	0	1	0	1
18.	0	0	0	0	0	0	0	0	0	0	0	0	0
	5	3	5	5	4	2	4	3	5	23	18	99	54

$\Sigma Gj_Y = 23$ $\Sigma Gj_J = 18$

$$Q_Y = (5\text{-}1)\ \frac{(5\ [5^2+3^2+5^2+5^2+5^2]\ \text{-}23^2)}{5(23)\text{-}99} = 4.00$$

$$Q_J = (5\text{-}1)\ \frac{(5\ [4^2+2^2+4^2+3^2+5^2]\ \text{-}18^2)}{5(18)\text{-}54} = 2.89$$

H_o = no significant difference between Yazbaki and Junblāṭṭi subgroups' fixed sorts and their analyzed free sorts

$df_Y = 5\text{-}1 = 4$
$p(\chi^2 \geqslant 9.49) = .05$
$4.00 < 9.49$

$df_J = 5\text{-}1 = 4$
$p(\chi^2 \geqslant 9.49) = .05$
$2.89 < 9.49$

Therefore, H_o can *not* be rejected.

BIBLIOGRAPHY

Abu Shaqra, H.
1952 The social movements in Lebanon (in Arabic). Beirut.

Alameddin, N.
1975 Druze marriage patterns. Unpublished M.A. thesis. American University of Beirut.

Armstrong, L. and G. Hirabayashi
1956 Social differentiation in selected Lebanese villages. American Sociological Review 21:425-34.

Asad, T.
1972 Market model, class structure and consent: a reconsideration of Swat political organization. Man 7(1):74-94.

Antoun, R.
1972 Arab village: a social structural study of a trans-Jordanian peasant community. Bloomington, Indiana: Indiana University Press.

Ayoub, M.
1957 Endogamous marriage in a Middle Eastern village. Unpublished Ph.D. dissertation. Harvard University.

Ayoub, V.
1955 Political structure of a Middle Eastern community: a Druze village of Mount Lebanon. Unpublished Ph.D. dissertation. Harvard University.
1965 Conflict resolution and social reorganization in a Lebanese village. Human Organization 24:11-17.
1966 Resolution of conflict in a Lebanese village. In: Politics in Lebanon, edited by L. Binder. New York: John Wiley and Sons.

Bashir, I.
1962 Planned administrative change in Lebanon. Beirut: American University of Beirut.

Bailey, F.
1972 Conceptual systems in the study of politics. In: Rural politics and social change in the Middle East, edited by R. Antoun and I. Harik. Bloomington, Indiana: Indiana University Press.

Barakat, H.
1973 Social and political integration in Lebanon: a case of social mosaic. Middle East Journal 27(3):301-18.

Barth, F.
1959*a* Segmentary opposition and the theory of games: a study of Pathan organization. Journal of the Royal Anthropological Institute of Great Britain and Ireland 89:5-21.
1959*b* Political leadership among Swat Pathans. London School of Economics Monographs on Social Anthropology, No. 19. London: The Athlone Press.

1960 The system of social stratification in Swat, north Pakistan. In: Aspects of caste in south India, Ceylon, and northwest Pakistan, edited by E. Leach. Cambridge, Great Britain: Cambridge University Press.
1961 Nomads of south Persia. Boston: Little, Brown and Company.
1963 The role of the entrepreneur in social change in northern Norway. Bergen, Norway: Scandinavian University Books.
1966 Models of social organization. Royal Anthropological Institute Occasional Papers, No. 23. Glasgow: The University Press.
1967 On the study of social change. American Anthropologist 69:661-69.
1969*a* Pathan identity and its maintenance. In: Ethnic groups and boundaries, edited by F. Barth. Boston: Little, Brown and Company.
1969*b* Introduction. In: Ethnic groups and boundaries, edited by F. Barth. Boston: Little, Brown and Company.
1972 Analytical dimensions in the comparison of social organizations. American Anthropologist 74:207-20.

Bennett, J.
1968 Paternalism. International Encyclopedia of the Social Sciences 15:472-77.

Berger, M.
1964 The Arab world today. Garden City, New York: Doubleday.

Berger, M.
1975 U.S. stops pistol sale to Lebanon. Washington Post, 23 July 1975.

Bernstein, B.
1964 Elaborated and restricted codes: their social origins and some consequences. American Anthropologist 66(6) Pt. 2:55-70.

Binder, L. (ed.)
1966 Politics in Lebanon. New York: John Wiley and Sons.

Blau, P.
1963 The dynamics of bureaucracy. (2nd ed.) Chicago: University of Chicago Press.
1964 Exchange and power in social life. New York: John Wiley and Sons.
1968 Social exchange. International Encyclopedia of the Social Sciences 7:452-57.
1971 Justice in social exchange. In: Institutions and social exchange, edited by H. Turk and R. Simpson. New York: Bobbs-Merrill.

Bouron, N.
1930 Les Druzes, histoire du Liban et de la Montagne Haouranaise. Paris.

Bryer, D.
1975 The origins of the Druze religion. Der Islam 52(1):47-84.

Conklin, H.
1955 Hanunóo color categories. Southwestern Journal of Anthropology 11: 339-44.
1962 The lexicographic treatment of folk taxonomies. In: Problems in lexicography, edited by F. Householder and S. Saporta. Bloomington, Indiana: Indiana University Press.
1964 Ethnogenealogical method. In: Explorations in cultural anthropology, edited by W. Goodenough. New York: McGraw-Hill.

Crow, R.
1966 Confessionalism, public administration, and efficiency in Lebanon. In: Politics in Lebanon, edited by L. Binder. New York: John Wiley and Sons.

De Sacy, S.
1838 Exposé de la religion des Druzes. 2 Vols. Paris.

De Vaumas, E.
1955 La répartition confessionelle au Liban et l'équilibre de l'état Libanaise. Revue de Géographie Alpine 43:511-604.

Farsoun, S.
1970 Family structure and society in modern Lebanon. In: Peoples and cultures of the Middle East, edited by L. Sweet, Vol. 2. Garden City, New York: The Natural History Press.

Firth, R.
1965 A note on mediators. Ethnology 4:386-88.

Fisher, W.
1971 The Middle East: a physical, social, and regional geography. (6th rev. ed.) London: Methuen and Company.

Frayha, A.
1956 Names of Lebanese cities and villages and a commentary on their meanings (in Arabic). Beirut: American University of Beirut.

Fredericks, R.
1974 Marriage patterns in a Lebanese village. Unpublished M.A. thesis. American University of Beirut.

Geertz, C.
1972 Summary comments. In: Rural politics and social change in the Middle East, edited by R. Antoun and I. Harik. Bloomington, Indiana: Indiana University Press.

Gellner, E.
1969 Saints of the Atlas. London: Weidenfeld and Nicolson.

Gubser, P.
1973 The *zu'amā'* of Zahlah: the current situation in a Lebanese town. Middle East Journal 27(2):173-89.

Gulick, J.
1955 Social structure and cultural change in a Lebanese village. New York: Wenner-Gren.
1968 The Arab Levant, an annotated bibliography. In: The central Middle East, edited by L. Sweet. New Haven, Connecticut: Human Relations Area Files.

Gulliver, P.
1969 Introduction to Part I. In: Law in culture and society, edited by L. Nader. Chicago: Aldine.

Gumperz, J.
1964 Linguistic and social interaction in two communities. American Anthropologist 66(6) Pt. 2:137-53.

Hakim, G.
1966 The economic basis of Lebanese polity. In: Politics in Lebanon, edited by L. Binder. New York: John Wiley and Sons.

Halpern, M.
1963 The politics of social change in the Middle East and North Africa. Princeton, New Jersey: Princeton University Press.

Harik, I.
1968 Politics and change in a traditional society. Princeton, New Jersey: Princeton University Press.
1972 The ethnic revolution and political integration in the Middle East. International Journal of Middle East Studies 3:303-23.
1974 The political mobilization of peasants. Bloomington, Indiana: Indiana University Press.

Hess, C. and H. Bodman, Jr.
1954 Confessionalism and feudality in Lebanese politics. Middle East Journal 8(1):10-26.

Hottinger, A.
1961 *Zu'amā'* and parties in the Lebanese crisis of 1958. Middle East Journal 15(2):127-40.

1966 *Zu'amā'* in historical perspective. In: Politics in Lebanon, edited by L. Binder. New York: John Wiley and Sons.

Hudson, M.
1968 The precarious republic. New York: Random House.

Huxley, F.
1972 A cross-linguistic study of semantic structure in English and Lebanese Colloquial Arabic. Unpublished M.A. thesis. American University of Beirut.

Hymes, D.
1964 Introduction: toward ethnographies of communication. American Anthropologist 66(6) Pt. 2:1-35.

Issawi, C.
1966 Economic development and political liberalism in Lebanon. In: Politics in Lebanon, edited by L. Binder. New York: John Wiley and Sons.

Johnson, S.
1967 Hierarchical clustering schemes. Psychometrika 32(3):241-54.

Joseph, S.
1975 The politicization of religious sects in Borj Hammond, Lebanon. Unpublished Ph.D. dissertation. Columbia University.

Kerr, M.
1966 Political decision-making in a confessional democracy. In: Politics in Lebanon, edited by L. Binder. New York: John Wiley and Sons.

Khalaf, S.
1968 Primordial ties and politics in Lebanon. Middle Eastern Studies 4:243-69.
1971 Family associations in Lebanon. Journal of Comparative Family Studies 2(2):235-50.
1974 Changing forms of political patronage in Lebanon (mimeo). Beirut: American University of Beirut.

Khuri, F.
1968 The etiquette of bargaining in the Middle East. American Anthropologist 70:698-706.
1969 The changing class structure in Lebanon. Middle East Journal 23(1):29-44.
1972 Sectarian loyalty among rural migrants in two Lebanese suburbs: a stage between family and national allegiance. In: Rural politics and social change in the Middle East, edited by R. Antoun and I. Harik. Bloomington, Indiana: Indiana University Press.
1975 From village to suburb: order and change in greater Beirut. Chicago: University of Chicago Press.

Kirk, G.
1964 A short history of the Middle East. (7th rev. ed.) New York: Praeger.

Kisrwani, M.
1971 Attitudes and behavior of Lebanese bureaucrats: a study in administrative corruption. Unpublished Ph.D. dissertation. Indiana University.

Lemarchand, R.
1972 Political clientalism and ethnicity in tropical Africa: competing solidarity in nation-building. American Political Science Review 68:68-90.

Lounsbury, F.
1955 The varieties of meaning. Georgetown University Monograph Series on Languages and Linguistics 8:158-64.
1956 A semantic analysis of Pawnee kinship usage. Language 32:158-94.
1963 Linguistics and psychology. In: Psychology: a study of a science, edited by S. Koch, Vol. 6. New York: McGraw-Hill.
1964*a* A formal account of the Crow- and Omaha-type kinship terminologies. In: Explorations in cultural anthropology, edited by W. Goodenough. New York: McGraw-Hill.
1964*b* The structural analysis of kinship semantics. In: Proceedings of the ninth international congress of linguists, edited by H. Hunt. The Hague: Mouton.

1965 Another view of the Trobriand kinship categories. American Anthropologist 67(5) Pt. 2:142-85.

Makarim, S.
1974 The Druze faith. Delmar, New York: Caravan.

Marchetti, V. and J. Marks
1974 The CIA and the cult of intelligence. New York: Dell.

Markham, J.
1975 In embattled Beirut, nerves are taut and the future is uncertain. New York Times, 19 July 1975.

Melikian, L. and L. Diab
1959 Group affiliations of university students in the Arab Middle East. Journal of Social Psychology 49:145-59.

Meo, L.
1965 Lebanon: improbable nation. Bloomington, Indiana: Indiana University Press.

Miller, C.
1978 *Wāsiṭa:* a multidimensional scaling model. Unpublished manuscript. University of California at Irvine.

Miller, G.
1967 Psycholinguistic approaches to the study of communication. In: Journeys in science, edited by D. Arms. Albuquerque, New Mexico: University of New Mexico Press.
1969 A psychological method to investigate verbal concepts. Journal of Mathematical Psychology 6:169-91.

Mintz, S.
1972 The plural society: perception and boundary building (mimeo). Paris: UNESCO.

Mirhij, A.
1972 Knowing Lebanon: the encyclopedia of Lebanese cities and villages (in Arabic), Vol. 3. Beirut: Lebanese People's Press.

Montagne, R.
1930 Les berbères et le makhzen dans le sud de Maroc. Paris.

Muller, G.
1972 Observation of a Lebanese village: Barouk (mimeo). Beirut.

Nader, L.
1962 A note on attitudes and the use of language. Anthropological Linguistics 4(6):24-29.
1965*a* Choices in Legal procedure: Shi'a Moslem and Mexican Zapotec. American Anthropologist 67:394-99.
1965*b* Communication between village and city in the modern Middle East. Human Organization 24:18-24.

Najjar, A.
n.d. The Druze (F. Massey, trans.). Atlanta, Georgia: American Druze Society.

Nicholas, R.
1965 Factions: a comparative analysis. In: Political systems and the distribution of power, edited by M. Banton. London: Tavistock.

Nordlinger, E.
1972 Conflict regulation in divided societies. Occasional Papers in International Affairs, No. 29. Cambridge, Massachusetts: Center for International Affairs, Harvard University.

Organization for Economic Cooperation and Development
1976 How income is distributed. New York Times, 10 September 1976.

Peters, E.
1970*a* Aspects of rank and status among Muslims in a Lebanese village. In: Peoples and cultures of the Middle East, edited by L. Sweet, Vol. 2. Garden City, New York: The Natural History Press.

1970*b* The proliferation of segments in the lineage of the Bedouin of Cyrenaica (Libya). In: Peoples and cultures of the Middle East, edited by L. Sweet, Vol. 1. Garden City, New York: The Natural History Press.
1972 Shifts in power in a Lebanese village. In: Rural politics and social change in the Middle East, edited by R. Antoun and I. Harik. Bloomington, Indiana: Indiana University Press.

Polk, W.
1963 The opening of south Lebanon, 1788-1840. Cambridge, Massachusetts: Harvard University Press.

Pospisil, L.
1965 A formal analysis of substantive law: Kapauku Papuan laws of land tenure. American Anthropologist 67(5) Pt. 2:186-214.
1971 Anthropology of law. New York: Harper and Row.

Powell, J.
1970 Peasant society and clientalist politics. American Political Science Review 64:411-25.

Prothro, E.
1961 Child rearing in the Lebanon. Cambridge, Massachusetts: Harvard University Press.

Qubain, F.
1961 Crisis in Lebanon. Washington, D.C.: Middle East Institute.

Rassam Vinogradov, A.
1974 The Ait Ndhir of Morocco: a study of the social transformation of a Berber tribe. Museum of Anthropology, University of Michigan, Anthropological Papers 55.

Rondot, P.
1954 Les structures socio-politiques de la nation libanaise. Revue Française de Science Politique 4:80-104.

Rosen, L.
1972 The social and conceptual framework of Arab-Berber relations in central Morocco. In: Arabs and Berbers, edited by E. Gellner and C. Micaud. Lexington, Massachusetts: D. C. Heath and Company.

Rothenberger, J.
1970 Law and conflict resolution, politics, and change in a Sunni Muslim village in Lebanon. Unpublished Ph.D. dissertation. University of California at Berkeley.

Salem, E.
1965 Local elections in Lebanon: a case study. Midwest Journal of Political Science 9:376-84.

Salibi, K.
1961 Lebanon since the crisis of 1958. The World Today 17(1):32-42.

Samaha, M.
1974 Wasta, or the gentle art of string pulling. Monday Morning, 21 April 1974.

Scheffler, H.
1966 Structuralism in anthropology. In: Structuralism, edited by J. Earmann. Yale French Studies, Nos. 36-37, 66-80.
1970 Review of C. Lévi-Strauss, the elementary structures of kinship. American Anthropologist 72:251-68.

Scheffler, H. and F. Lounsbury
1971 A study in structural semantics: the Siriono kinship system. Englewood Cliffs, New Jersey: Prentice-Hall.

Scott, J.
1972 Patron-client politics and political change in southeast Asia. American Political Science Review 66:91-113.

Seddon, J. D.
1969 Kinship, friendship, and factions. Annales Marocaines de Sociologie. Rabat.
1972 Local politics and state intervention: northeast Morocco from 1870 to 1970. In: Arabs and Berbers, edited by E. Gellner and C. Micaud. Lexington, Massachusetts: D. C. Heath Company.

Silverman, S.
1965 Patronage and community-nation relationships in central Italy. Ethnology 4:172-89.
1966 An ethnographic approach to social stratification: prestige in a central Italian community. American Anthropologist 68:899-921.

Similianskaya, I.
1966 From subsistence to market economy, 1850's. In: The economic history of the Middle East, 1800-1914, edited by C. Issawi. Chicago: University of Chicago Press.

Skvoretz, J. and R. Conviser
1972 Exchange and alliances: a reformulation of Barth's models of social organization (mimeo). University of Pittsburgh, Pittsburgh, Pennsylvania.

Sokal, R. and P. Sneath
1963 Principles of numerical taxonomy. San Francisco and London: W. H. Freeman.

Suleiman, M.
1965 Political parties in Lebanon. Ithaca, New York: Cornell University Press.

Sweet, L.
1967 The women of Ain ad-Dayr. Anthropological Quarterly 40:167-83.
1974 Visiting patterns and social dynamics in a Lebanese Druze village. Anthropological Quarterly 47(10):112-19.

Tannous, A.
1942 Group behavior in the village community of Lebanon. American Journal of Sociology 63(2):231-39.

Touma, T.
1971 Paysans et institutions féodales chez les Druzes et les Maronites du Liban du XVIIe siècle à 1914, Vol. 1. Beirut: Lebanese University.

Turner, J.
1974 The structure of sociological theory. Homewood, Illinois: Dorsey Press.

U.S. Department of State
1975 Background notes: Lebanon. Washington, D.C.: U.S. Government Printing Office.

Wehr, H.
1961 A dictionary of modern written Arabic. Ithaca, New York: Cornell University Press.

Williams, H. and J. R. Williams
1965 The extended family as a vehicle of culture change. Human Organization 24(1):59-64.

Wolf, E.
1956 Aspects of group relations in a complex society: Mexico. American Anthropologist 58:1065-77.
1966*a* Peasants. Englewood Cliffs, New Jersey: Prentice-Hall.
1966*b* Kinship, friendship, and patron-client relations in complex societies. In: The social anthropology of complex societies, edited by M. Banton. London: Tavistock.

Yaukey, D.
1961 Fertility differences in a modernizining country: a survey of Lebanese couples. Princeton, New Jersey: Princeton University Press.

Zecher, L.
1967 The men of influence and the exercise of influence in Nabatieh, Lebanon. Unpublished M.A. thesis. American University of Beirut.

Zenner, W. and M. Richter, Jr.
1972 The Druzes as a divided minority group. Journal of Asian and African Studies 7(3/4):193-203.

Zuwiyya, J.
1972 The parliamentary election of Lebanon: 1968. Leiden, Holland: E. J. Brill.

Zuwiyya-Yamak, L.
1966 Party politics in the Lebanese political system. In: Politics in Lebanon, edited by L. Binder. New York: John Wiley and Sons.

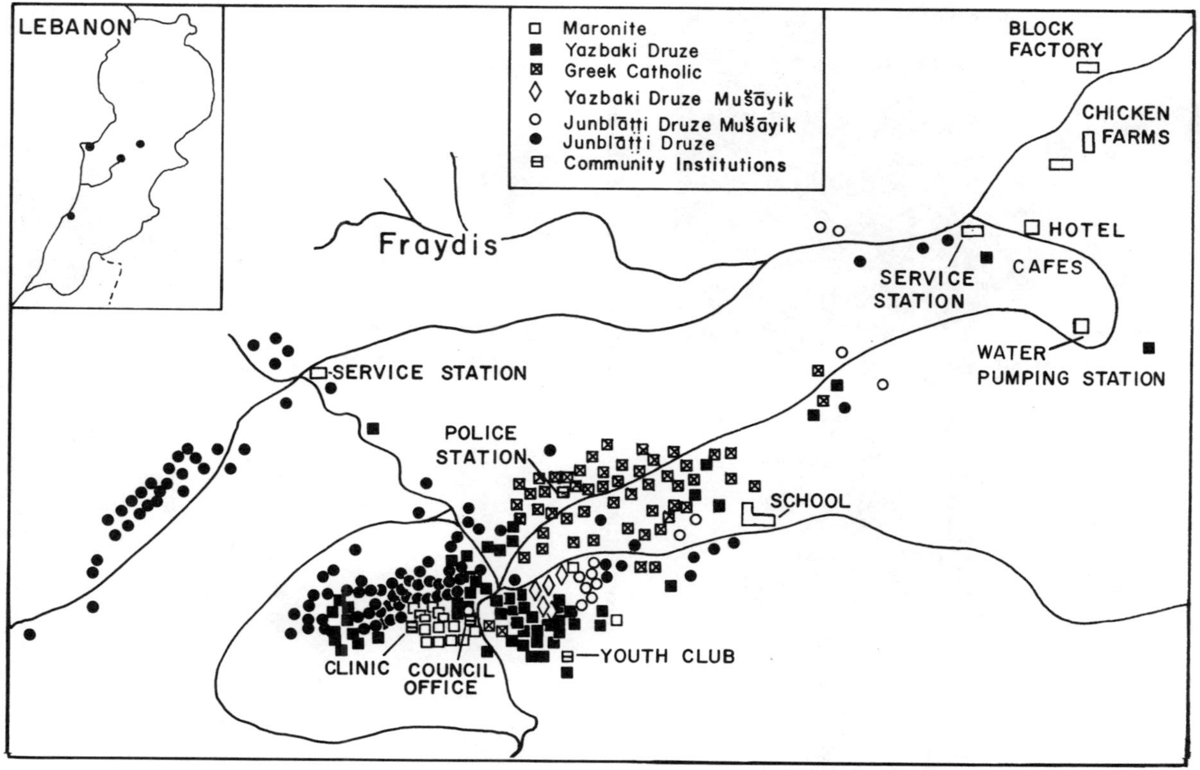

Map of the village of Barouk, indicating residential locations of the different population subgroups.

Plate 1. A friend standing before the neighboring village of Fraydis.

Plate 2. A young man before the pine and cedar groves.

Plate 3. A summertime wedding procession through the market.

Plate 4. Making *'araq*.

Plate 5. Druze *'ajawīd* ladies walking through the market in early morning.